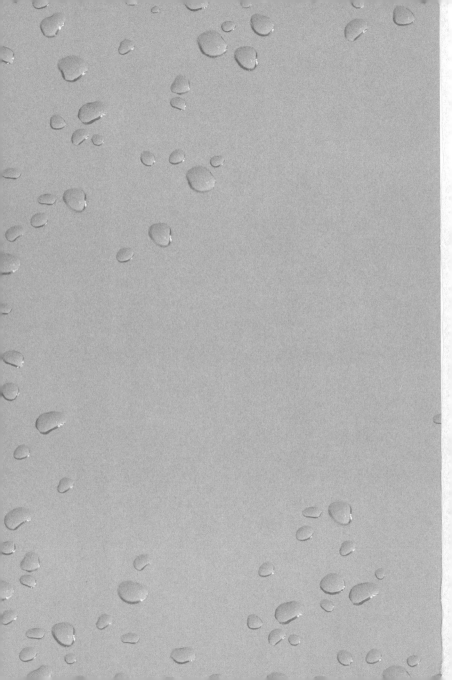

START with PRAYER

250 PRAYERS FOR HOPE AND STRENGTH

MAX LUCADO

with *Andrea Lucado, Betsy St. Amant,*
Jennifer K. Hale, and Mark Mynheir

THOMAS NELSON
Since 1798

Start with Prayer
© 2022 Max Lucado

Portions of this book were adapted from: *Pocket Prayers, Pocket Prayers for Moms, Pocket Prayers for Dads, Pocket Prayers for Friends, Pocket Prayers for Graduates, Pocket Prayers for Military,* and *Pocket Prayers for Teachers.*

All rights reserved. No portion of this book may be reproduced, stored in a retrieval system, or transmitted in any form or by any means—electronic, mechanical, photocopy, recording, scanning, or other—except for brief quotations in critical reviews or articles, without the prior written permission of the publisher.

Published in Nashville, Tennessee, by Thomas Nelson. Thomas Nelson is a registered trademark of HarperCollins Christian Publishing, Inc.

Thomas Nelson titles may be purchased in bulk for educational, business, fundraising, or sales promotional use. For information, please e-mail SpecialMarkets@ThomasNelson.com.

All Scripture quotations, unless otherwise indicated, are taken from the New King James Version˙ (NKJV). Copyright © 1982 by Thomas Nelson. Used by permission. All rights reserved.

Other Scripture references are from the following sources:

Scripture quotations marked CEB are taken from the Common English Bible. Copyright © 2011 Common English Bible.

Scripture quotations marked ESV are taken from the ESV˙ Bible (The Holy Bible, English Standard Version˙). Copyright © 2001 by Crossway, a publishing ministry of Good News Publishers. Used by permission. All rights reserved.

Scripture quotations marked THE MESSAGE are taken from *THE MESSAGE.* Copyright © 1993, 2002, 2018 by Eugene H. Peterson. Used by permission of NavPress. All rights reserved. Represented by Tyndale House Publishers, Inc.

Scripture quotations marked NCV are taken from the New Century Version˙. Copyright © 2005 by Thomas Nelson. Used by permission. All rights reserved.

Scripture quoted by permission. Quotations designated (NET©) are from the NET Bible˙ copyright ©1996–2017 by Biblical Studies Press, L.L.C. http://netbible.com. All rights reserved.

Scripture quotations taken from The Holy Bible, New International Version˙, NIV˙. Copyright © 1973, 1978, 1984, 2011 by Biblica, Inc.˙ Used by permission of Zondervan. All rights reserved worldwide. www.Zondervan.com. The "NIV" and "New International Version" are trademarks registered in the United States Patent and Trademark Office by Biblica, Inc.˙

Scripture quotations marked NLT are taken from the Holy Bible, New Living Translation. © 1996, 2004, 2015 by Tyndale House Foundation. Used by permission of Tyndale House Publishers, Inc., Carol Stream, Illinois 60188. All rights reserved.

Scripture quotations marked TLB are taken from The Living Bible. Copyright © 1971. Used by permission of Tyndale House Publishers, Inc., Carol Stream, Illinois 60188. All rights reserved.

ISBN 978-1-4016-0647-3 (audiobook)
ISBN 978-1-4016-0646-6 (eBook)
ISBN 978-1-4016-0378-6 (HC)

Printed in the United States of America

22 23 24 25 26   LSC   10 9 8 7 6 5 4 3 2 1

CONTENTS

Also by Max Lucado

ACKNOWLEDGMENTS

I'm offering a prayer of deep gratitude and my personal admiration for the team who contributed exceptional skill and creativity to this volume of prayers:

Michael Briggs, Angela Guzman, Jennifer K. Hale, Andrea Lucado, Mark Mynheir, Betsy St. Amant, Karen Hill, and Janene MacIvor.

And a special thanks to all the readers who have prayed for me and my family through the years. No gift is greater than the gift of your prayers. My gratitude is unending.

INTRODUCTION

Moses prayed, and the Red Sea opened.

Abraham prayed, and Lot's family was spared.

Elijah prayed, and fire fell.

Joshua prayed, and the walls of Jericho collapsed.

Nehemiah prayed, and the walls of Jerusalem were rebuilt.

The disciples prayed, and the church was born.

The church prayed, and Peter was freed.

Peter and Cornelius prayed, and the gospel was taken to the world.

Do you think things happen when people pray? Yes!

"God will always give what is right to his people who cry to him night and day. . . I tell you, God will help his people quickly" (Luke 18:7–8 NCV).

"When two of you get together on anything at all on earth and make a prayer out of it, my

1

Father in heaven goes into action" (Matt. 18:19 THE MESSAGE).

"And we are sure of this, that he will listen to us whenever we ask him for anything in line with his will" (1 John 5:14 TLB).

Is any other spiritual activity promised such power? Did Jesus call us to preach without ceasing? Or teach without ceasing? Or have committee meetings without ceasing? Or sing without ceasing? No, but he did call us to "pray without ceasing" (1 Thess. 5:17).

God is moved by the humble, prayerful heart. "The LORD will hear your crying and he will comfort you. When he hears you, he will help you" (Isa. 30:19 NCV).

We can do much after we pray. But we should do nothing before we pray. Let's start with prayer.

PRAYERS *for* CLARITY AND CREATIVITY

1

God is not the author of confusion but of peace.

1 CORINTHIANS 14:33

Father, your love is perfect, and your ways are perfect. I cannot begin to understand the depths of your love and wisdom.

Help me to be wise. As I need to make decisions, give me clarity and peace. You are not a God of confusion, so I want to hear your voice alone.

Please bring peace to me as I make choices. Keep me far from confused thoughts and close to your perfect peace.

Thank you for direction and guidance. You always provide for me.

In the name of my true Provider, amen.

2

For God has not given us a spirit of fear, but of
power and of love and of a sound mind.

F ather, you are all-powerful, all-knowing, and
almighty. You can move mountains and do wonders
beyond my imagination.

Be with me today when I begin to fear. Remind me
that fear is not of you, and replace my fear with peace and
love and a sound mind—with clarity.

Walk closely with my loved ones today as they go in
their own directions. Don't let them be overcome by fear
or doubt, but instead fill them with a sense of your love.

Thank you that I never have a reason to fear, for you
have given me the strength to meet any challenge today.

In your name I pray, amen.

3

Be strong and of good courage . . . do not fear nor
be dismayed, for the LORD God—my God—will be
with you. He will not leave you nor forsake you.

1 CHRONICLES 28:20

Heavenly Father, you are the Lord of all, the almighty God, and the everlasting one.

Be near to me when I face change. When nothing feels steady, it is hard on me. Give me strength and courage in times of transition.

Allow me to see you leading the way. May I rely on you, especially when I feel uncertain.

I am so grateful that even when everything around me feels unstable, you are there. You are my rock. I thank you and praise you for that.

In Christ's name, amen.

4

Let us therefore come boldly to the throne
of grace, that we may obtain mercy and
find grace to help in time of need.

HEBREWS 4:16

Father, you hear every prayer, and you see every face. You care about your children, including me.

I'm asking today for clarity. I so often try to figure things out on my own, but right now I'll stop trying. I surrender my life to you.

As I surrender my life, I surrender my loved ones' lives as well. They are yours. Help them approach you with boldness so that they can know your grace.

Thank you that you've promised help in my time of need.

In Jesus' name, amen.

5

That the God of our Lord Jesus Christ, the Father
of glory, may give to you the spirit of wisdom and
revelation in the knowledge of Him, the eyes of
your understanding being enlightened; that you
may know what is the hope of His calling.

EPHESIANS 1:17-18

God, you are good. Evil trembles in your presence. It is no match for your power and for your love.

Sometimes I get lost in my various roles in life. Remind me today that my identity is found in you.

Remind my family that there is hope in your calling, that you have a plan for each of their lives, and that it includes loving others as you have loved each of us.

Thank you for the incredible privilege of being your child. What joy and love you bring to my life.

In your name I pray, amen.

6

If any of you lacks wisdom,
let him ask of God,
who gives to all liberally and without reproach,
and it will be given to him.

JAMES 1:5

God, you are Jehovah-jireh, the giver of everything. You take care of me even before I can ask for help.

You gave me my talents. When I am feeling uninspired and need new ideas, reignite the passion in me. Give me wisdom, and help me use my imagination to create new ways to reach my potential. Let me be an effective follower of Christ by using my gifts from you.

Help my supporting circle tap into their talents and use them well. Let your glory shine in their skills so we can celebrate the achievement of our efforts through your mighty work.

Thank you for the talents you've so generously poured on my friends and me. Thank you for abilities that make us diverse and beautiful in your eyes.

In Jesus' name, amen.

7

The entrance of Your words gives light;
it gives understanding to the simple.

PSALM 119:130

Father in heaven, you speak all things into being. You create life with your words, and they bring light to the darkness.

Lord, bring light to my darkness today. The future can feel scary and is filled with the unknown. When my mind strays to anxious thoughts, light a path back to clarity and peace.

May your light enter my family today and bring understanding. Some of my family members are still learning to trust in you, and I don't want them to fear the future. Give them peace and clear direction today.

Thank you for answering my prayers.

In Christ's name, amen.

8

The fear of the LORD is the instruction of wisdom,
And before honor is humility.

PROVERBS 15:33

My God in heaven, I praise you, for you alone are worthy of praise.

Sometimes I get too caught up in the details of my life. Help me remember that I have no idea what goes on in the homes of my colleagues. Give me ears to listen and eyes to see. Let me learn from them, and remind me that their life experiences, although different from mine, are valuable.

Protect my work family, Lord. When they leave me, go with them. Open their hearts so we can learn from one another. Help them learn more than facts, help them learn values and the beginnings of wisdom.

Thank you for all my colleagues and their families.

In Christ's name, amen.

9

Add to your faith virtue, to virtue knowledge,
to knowledge self-control,
to self-control perseverance, to perseverance godliness,
to godliness brotherly kindness,
and to brotherly kindness love.
For if these things are yours and abound,
you will be neither barren nor unfruitful.

2 PETER 1:5–8

Mighty God, you are good. You give strength, knowledge, wisdom, and mercy in abundance, and my cup runs over.

I want to be an effective follower of Christ. I want to pass on not only knowledge but also your love to my friends, letting them see you through my creativity. Let me be productive in my work. Help my colleagues excel in their hard work.

Bless our community. Unify us; give us common goals. Help us get along and love one another so we can work together well to serve our community.

Thank you for loving and giving. Thank you for pouring yourself into my life. Your mercy is my strength.

In your name, amen.

10

There is a time for everything,
and a season for every activity under the heavens:

a time to be born and a time to die,
a time to plant and a time to uproot,
a time to kill and a time to heal,
a time to tear down and a time to build,
a time to weep and a time to laugh.

ECCLESIASTES 3:1–4 NIV

God, you are the ultimate timekeeper. You have mapped the perfect plan for our lives and know the number of our days.

Help me discern good timing—to know the time for firm discipline in my home and the time for laughter, to recognize when I need a listening ear and open arms and when my family needs advice and counsel.

Help me remember the importance of a willingness to learn. Please help me create goals that will serve as motivation.

Thank you for your plans, for they are greater than ours.

In your eternal name, amen.

11

Instruct the wise and they will be wiser still;
teach the righteous and they will add to their learning.

PROVERBS 9:9 NIV

F ather in heaven, you are the source of all knowledge, the provider of all things great and small.

Please give me a mentor—someone who can provide ideas and techniques that will make me a better worker. Remind me why I chose my profession. Give me a heart willing to listen and the ability to mentor someone else in the future.

As others near retirement, bless their work. Instill in them the desire to mentor newer workers and to pass on their strategies and plans, helping newer professionals impact lives for coming generations.

Thank you for the wisdom of talented teachers, mentors, and advisors. Thank you for making me a lifelong student, seeking you most of all, Father.

In Christ's name, amen.

12

Whoever gives heed to instruction prospers,
and blessed is the one who trusts in the LORD.

PROVERBS 16:20 NIV

Jesus, your teaching instructs my heart and soul. There is no one greater than you.

Make me eager to listen to and learn from others. Sometimes professional development seems unnecessary, but give me a willing heart to learn and to apply new ideas to my career so I can grow.

Give my company the ability to see when employees need more encouragement and help in order to make our business stronger.

Thank you for being the example of the ultimate leader. Thank you for mercy and grace and for showing us the value of living each day by walking in the ways you've laid out for us.

In your holy name, amen.

13

*God is able to bless you abundantly, so that
in all things at all times, having all that you
need, you will abound in every good work.*

2 CORINTHIANS 9:8 NIV

God, through your gifts you pour your unending love over us. You bless us so we can bless others.

Please give me clarity of mind and an extra dose of creativity when I'm focusing on my work plans and projects. Help me see each person as you do: unique.

Give me a heart to serve, energy to explore new ideas, and wisdom to follow your leading.

Thank you for blessing me. Thank you for your goodness and your mercy. And thank you for each day and each lesson of life.

In your name, amen.

14

Let my teaching fall like rain and my words
descend like dew, like showers on new grass,
like abundant rain on tender plants.

DEUTERONOMY 32:2 NIV

Father, your words are the foundation of my heart's belief. You are the rock on which I depend.

Help me stay engaged each day by capturing my attention, piquing my curiosity, fueling my desire to learn, and encouraging participation. Let your words water my thirsty mind and your love help me grow relationships with others.

Give me a passion for engagement and the drive to use the gifts you've given me to make a difference. Help me use words of encouragement to foster growth.

Thank you that the Holy Spirit engages me through your Word and that your promises cover me like soft rain.

In Jesus' name, amen.

PRAYERS *for* CONVICTION

15

*Fight the good fight of faith, lay hold on eternal life,
to which you were also called and have confessed the
good confession in the presence of many witnesses.*

1 TIMOTHY 6:12

Father, you are fighting for me. You won the war over sin, and now you reign in my heart as the King of my life.

There are days when my eyes drift away from you. Some people pressure me to do things I don't want to do, and it's hard to say no. Keep me focused on you and the purpose you have for me.

Please help me "fight the good fight of faith." Don't let me get distracted, but help me stand strong in your Word.

Thank you for being the Rock on which I can stand.

In Jesus' name, amen.

16

*Therefore submit to God. Resist the devil
and he will flee from you. Draw near to
God and He will draw near to you.*

JAMES 4:7–8

Dear God, you are the creator of everything beautiful in the world, including the mountains, oceans, rivers, and seasons. And yet you want to have a relationship with me, your child.

Draw near to me, God. Be close to me so I don't stumble into sin. It is easy to do that in this fallen world.

I'm worried about people in my family who are not following you and don't seem to have much faith. Please remind them today of your love.

Thank you for sending your Son so we can always be near you.

In Jesus' name, amen.

17

*Stand therefore, having girded your waist with truth,
having put on the breastplate of righteousness, and
having shod your feet with the preparation of the gospel
of peace; above all, taking the shield of faith with
which you will be able to quench all the fiery darts of
the wicked one. And take the helmet of salvation, and
the sword of the Spirit, which is the word of God.*

EPHESIANS 6:14–17

Father, you are truth, righteousness, and peace. With you, anything is possible. No problem is too big for you to solve.

Sometimes I have a hard time standing up for what I believe. No one around me seems to care about you. Strengthen me each day to live in your truth.

Be with the people I encounter today, especially those who don't know you. Help me model you in all I do.

Your Word assures me you are my provider. Thank you for being with me no matter where I am.

In Christ's name I pray, amen.

18

For the world offers only a craving for physical pleasure,
a craving for everything we see, and pride in our
achievements and possessions. These are not from the
Father, but are from this world. And this world is fading
away, along with everything that people crave. But
anyone who does what pleases God will live forever.

1 JOHN 2:16-17 NLT

Dear God, you are holy and deserve all the glory. Sometimes I feel unsure about my beliefs because of the influences around me. Give me confidence in my faith, Lord. I don't want to be like the world. I want to be like Jesus.

I pray for our church leaders. When people come to them with doubts and questions, please give them the words to say that will encourage them.

Thank you for my church and the people who taught me to love and believe in you.

In Jesus' name, amen.

19

For am I now seeking the approval of man, or of God? . . .
If I were still trying to please man,
I would not be a servant of Christ.

GALATIANS 1:10 ESV

Dear Father, you are always the same. No matter what I do or say, your love never changes.

Forgive me for the times I have been embarrassed about my Christian faith. I want people to like me so badly sometimes, but I know you are the only one I need to please, and I know you care about me.

Please give me the courage to speak up for you, to be bold in faith, kind in speech, and thoughtful in actions.

Thank you for the blessings in my life. There are so many.

In Jesus' name, amen.

20

For those who live according to the flesh set their minds on the things of the flesh, but those who live according to the Spirit, the things of the Spirit. For to be carnally minded is death, but to be spiritually minded is life and peace.

ROMANS 8:5-6

God, you give me grace every day. You never run out. I can count on your grace for the rest of my life.

On days that are busy and challenging, help me focus on everything that is peaceful and good and life giving.

Help me find hope and peace when I read your Word today. Guide me toward reading scriptures that you want me to dwell on.

Thank you for the gift of peace.

In Christ I pray, amen.

21

Do not forget my law,
But let your heart keep my commands;
For length of days and long life
And peace they will add to you.
Let not mercy and truth forsake you;
Bind them around your neck,
Write them on the tablet of your heart.

PROVERBS 3:1-3

Dear God, you are the only judge. You are the one who knows my heart through and through.

I am learning so many new things in life. Let me consider all new things in the light of your Word and who you want me to be. Write your Word on my heart.

I pray for my family and friends who don't believe in you. Show them who you are and how much you love and care for them.

Thank you for each new truth you reveal to me about you and your creation.

In Jesus' name, amen.

PRAYERS *for*
COURAGE

22

Greater love has no one than this,
than to lay down one's life
for his friends.

JOHN 15:13

God, you are the supreme warrior. Your mighty hands will bring true justice and peace to the world in your good time.

Lord, I believe in you. Please strengthen my spirit, my mind, and my body so I can serve you well and bring glory to your name. Remind me that I am secure in you no matter what. Enable me to put the needs of my friends and the people in my life ahead of my own. Let them see you in my actions.

Please give peace and comfort to my loved ones and friends. Remind them that our lives are in your loving hands.

Thank you for strengthening me and showing me true love through your Son's sacrifice.

In Jesus' name, amen.

23

Have I not commanded you? Be strong and of good courage; do not be afraid, nor be dismayed, for the LORD your God is with you wherever you go.

JOSHUA 1:9

Lord, your strength and authority are without limits. You cast out all fear, and you fill your people with boldness and power.

Help me, Lord, not to be gripped and controlled by fear. When frightening times come, please remind me that you are with me. Set my eyes and my heart on your promise that you will never leave me or forsake me. Help me trust you with my very life so I can live without fear or hesitation. Go before me like a light; shine in the dark places I may be called to enter.

Please be with my family and chase their fears away too. Comfort them and give them peace when I'm absent.

Thank you for being with me today and every day. I am grateful for your promises and your guidance.

In your Son's holy name, amen.

24

The LORD is my strength and my shield;
My heart trusted in Him, and I am helped;
Therefore my heart greatly rejoices,
And with my song I will praise Him.

PSALM 28:7

Father, you never leave us. You never forsake us. You are the God who protects his people. You are worthy of all praise and honor.

I confess, Lord, that I rely too often on my own strength. Remind me to trust you first and foremost. Help me place my entire faith and hope in you as my shield and my strength. Teach me to pray and follow your Spirit and rely on you.

When things seem dark and overwhelming, remind me to run to your shelter of protection, comfort, and love. Teach me to lean on you during those times.

Thank you for going ahead of me into uncertain times. Thank you for covering me and my family with your power and your truth.

In Christ's name, amen.

25

Be of good courage, and let us be strong for our people and for the cities of our God. And may the Lord do what is good in His sight.

2 SAMUEL 10:12

Heavenly Father, you know the hearts and intentions of all people, and your justice is perfect and righteous. Your plans will reign supreme.

I yearn for peace but prepare my heart for challenging times that come with any life. Guide my spirit to be steadfast and courageous so I can step up to these challenges and shine your light to others during hard times.

I want to be courageous even when my immediate family is struggling. Help them also understand and be able to manage the difficult days. Reassure them that the safest path is to follow your will.

Thank you for the privilege of being your child. I am so grateful for every day and that your love is a constant through the ups and downs of this life.

In your name, amen.

26

I long to see you so that I may impart to you some
spiritual gift to make you strong—that is, that you and
I may be mutually encouraged by each other's faith.

ROMANS 1:11-12 NIV

Gracious Father, you are the Great Deliverer and my true salvation. You parted a sea and walked your people through it. Nothing is beyond your mighty reach.

Help me remember this when I face challenges, and grant me the wisdom to know when to lean on others for strength and encouragement.

Thank you for the people in my community who give me the courage to face each new day with resolve. I am particularly grateful for the spiritual mentors and church leaders you've placed in my life.

Please protect them and all my friends who stand up for our beliefs. Bless the incredible people whom you have allowed me to call my community. May I always be faithful to you and to them.

In your holy name, amen.

27

Yea, though I walk through the valley of the shadow of death,
I will fear no evil;
For You are with me;
Your rod and Your staff, they comfort me.

PSALM 23:4

God, you have given us the Comforter. You ease the concerns of your people. Death has no power, because of your gift of eternal life through the redeeming gift of your Son's sacrifice.

Lord, if I find myself challenged by evil, I pray you will go ahead of me and build a hedge of protection around me.

I am thankful for the gift of your love and care. Thank you for being with me every day, in every situation, as I do my best to honor my commitment to you.

In Jesus' name, amen.

28

I heard the voice of the Lord, saying:
"Whom shall I send,
And who will go for Us?"
Then I said, "Here am I! Send me."

ISAIAH 6:8

Holy, holy, holy are you, Lord Almighty. You are high above all people. Let them praise your name forever.

I am here, Lord. Send me—not just in my job but in my life. I haven't always made myself fully available to you and your will. Please forgive me and change my heart so I will go where you would have me go and stay where you would have me stay. I do not want to hold back from you in any part of my life.

Let the spirit of my home be bold and strong in faith.

Thank you for guiding my steps and placing me where you have. I am grateful for the opportunities to serve you today and tomorrow and beyond.

In your mighty name, amen.

29

The LORD is my light and my salvation;
Whom shall I fear?
The LORD is the strength of my life;
Of whom shall I be afraid?

PSALM 27:1

Father, you are the light of the world and the hope of all people. You strengthen those who follow you. You are our hope and our salvation!

Calm my fears and worries today. Help me stay focused on you and what's important in my life. I get caught up in worrying about small things that really don't matter, especially in view of your salvation. Help me rest in your promises and just trust you.

Light the way for my family today. When they start to fret over daily concerns, remind them that you love them and watch over them at all times.

Thank you for keeping fear and worry from having a grip on our lives. I am so thankful you care about the small things as well as the large ones.

In your Son's name, amen.

30

The LORD is near to all who call upon Him,
To all who call upon Him in truth.

PSALM 145:18

Dear God, you are the Alpha and Omega, the beginning and the end of all things. You are worthy of all praise and honor.

Even though sometimes I feel so far away from you, help me know that you are always right here beside me. And help me to call on you in truth and to seek you with my whole heart. I'm thankful I'm not walking through this life without you.

Draw my family close to you today so they can feel your presence. Help my loved ones learn to call on you always. Teach them to pray more and to rely on you.

Thank you for choosing to be with your creation and for loving us so much. I praise you for desiring a relationship with us.

In Jesus' name, amen.

31

I am not ashamed of the gospel of Christ, for it is the
power of God to salvation for everyone who believes.

ROMANS 1:16

Lord, by your name alone are people saved. Your unfailing love built the bridge from you to us. Your love conquers all.

Help me be bold with my faith and unashamed that I follow you so I will speak freely about you. Help me walk in courage and faith every day because my strength and dependence flow from the Holy Spirit. Provide opportunities for me to share your love with my friends and coworkers, and give me the heart to stand strong for you. Teach me how to be an example for my children.

Bless my family, Lord, so they will know you and will want to tell others about you. Give them an excitement and a deep joy in serving you. Fill our home with your strength and courage.

Thank you for strengthening our hearts and our resolve to follow you without apprehension or wavering.

In your Son's name, amen.

32

"Not by might nor by power, but by My Spirit,"
Says the LORD of hosts.

ZECHARIAH 4:6

Father, by your Spirit the world was created and is sustained. By your Spirit you lead and guide your people. I praise your holy name.

As I face obstacles, fears, and temptations, please guide me to rely on you. Point me to scriptures that will give me the courage and strength to face the day. Give me a humble attitude so I will simply listen to you and follow your leading.

Direct my family today. Show us your loving grace and wisdom. Protect us and let peace sweep across my home as we learn to rely on you and not ourselves.

Thank you for sending your Spirit to lead, comfort, and protect us. Thank you for loving my family more than I ever could.

In Jesus' name, amen.

33

*I have told you these things, so that in me you may
have peace. In this world you will have trouble.
But take heart! I have overcome the world.*

JOHN 16:33 NIV

God, your peace surpasses all understanding, and your mercies are new every morning. Your majesty flows over all the earth.

Sometimes I feel as if my troubles are about to overwhelm me. I feel trapped by worry and fear. Help me have your peace and your assurance that you have already overcome all my concerns. Forgive me for not trusting you as I should. Steady my faith.

Walk closely with my family today. Wrap your arms around them, and calm their hearts so they aren't overcome by anxiety or dread.

Thank you that you have already defeated any future troubles, believing that you stand ready to give strength for each day. I am deeply thankful for the encouragement of your promises.

In your Son's name, amen.

34

And we know that all things work together
for good to those who love God, to those who
are the called according to His purpose.

ROMANS 8:28

Dear God, you are great and mighty. You planned and purposed every moment of every life on earth. You know all and control all. You are Lord of all!

Remind me today that when unexpected, troublesome, or even painful things enter my life, you have allowed them for my benefit—to strengthen me. Help me to appreciate the difficulties and challenges and to have the proper attitude toward them.

As my children learn more about you and your ways, help them realize you want only good for them. Teach them to pray and walk with you through the good times and bad. Reinforce their faith today.

Thank you for weaving the events and circumstances in our lives to fit into your amazing plan. I am grateful that your plan includes my family.

In Christ's name, amen.

35

Believe on the Lord Jesus Christ,
and you will be saved,
you and your household.

ACTS 16:31

Lord, you are all-knowing and all powerful. Heaven is your throne, and the earth is your footstool.

I wonder sometimes if I'm teaching my family about you as I should. Guide me to be a godly person so I can be the kind of nurturer you want me to be. Break down any barriers that keep me from being that person.

Show my family that your ways are best. Create in each of us a desire to follow you so we will love you with all our hearts, all our minds, and all our souls.

I am so grateful I can come to you on behalf of my family. Thank you for carefully watching over them and leading them to you.

In your holy name, amen.

PRAYERS *for*
FRIENDSHIP

36

For God did not appoint us to wrath, but to obtain
salvation through our Lord Jesus Christ, who died
for us, that whether we wake or sleep, we should
live together with Him. Therefore comfort each other
and edify one another, just as you also are doing.

1 THESSALONIANS 5:9-11

Father, my relationship with you is the most important one in my life. You matter more than anyone or anything else. But I am tempted to put my earthly relationships before you, God. Forgive me. Remind me to put you first in my life always.

Help me set aside the things of the world that pull me away from you, Lord. Thank you for your Word and for all the ways I hear your voice when I read your holy Word.

Thank you for creating me and wanting a relationship with me.

In your name I pray, amen.

37

Each of you should use whatever gift you have received
to serve others, as faithful stewards of God's grace in
its various forms. . . . If anyone serves, they should
do so with the strength God provides, so that in all
things God may be praised through Jesus Christ.

1 PETER 4:10–11 NIV

Almighty God, I praise you for your good heart toward your children. Even when I fail, your love never does. You are worthy to be praised.

Help me to be mindful of my motives. When I serve others, let it be out of genuine kindness and not selfishness, giving you all the glory. I want to set an example and encourage others toward good works. Help me show my friends true love and humility.

Please be with my friends as they strive to live for you. Help them stir one another toward good things. Let their hearts be focused on you alone.

Thank you that your love for me doesn't depend on my works but on your grace alone. Thank you for my friends, who remind me with their wisdom and joy of your many blessings. I'm so grateful we can work together and bring you glory.

In your holy and precious Son's name, amen.

38

He who walks with wise men will be wise,
But the companion of fools will be destroyed.

PROVERBS 13:20

Almighty God, you sent your Son as an example of love, holiness, and wisdom. I praise you for that.

Help me reflect your love and embrace the wisdom you offer. I ask you to bring healthy friendships into my life and to protect me from relationships that would pull me away from you.

Bring positive influences into the lives of my friends. Equip them to sharpen one another to become more like you every day.

Thank you for caring about every aspect of my life, especially the people in it. And thank you for continuing to open doors to relationships that honor you.

In the name of Jesus, amen.

39

Do not be deceived: "Evil company corrupts good habits."

1 CORINTHIANS 15:33

Heavenly Father, I praise you for your constant involvement in my life. You never fail to meet all my needs and to lead me in truth.

I need discernment today regarding the friendships I allow in my life. Give me wisdom to know which relationships to embrace and which ones to pass by.

I ask you to guide my friends in this too. Protect them from negative influences that might draw them away from your presence.

Thank you for being a constant friend. Even in temporary seasons of loneliness, you're with me. I'm so grateful for your presence when other relationships are in transition.

In Jesus' name, amen.

40

He said to me, "My grace is sufficient for you, for
my power is made perfect in weakness." Therefore I
will boast all the more gladly about my weaknesses,
so that Christ's power may rest on me.

2 CORINTHIANS 12:9 NIV

Dear Lord, you alone are worthy. You're the only one who can meet me exactly where I am. Your grace is all I truly need.

Some days I struggle to embrace that truth even though I believe it. I need help holding on to you when circumstances try to convince me otherwise. Give me wisdom to understand your power, grace, and provision in the days they feel out of reach.

Help my friends recognize your provision even in the hard times. Let them always sense your presence, support, and love. Pour your grace into their lives, and make them strong.

Thank you for always meeting my needs, just as your Word promises. On the days when my patience runs thin and my heart breaks, your grace is still enough to cover all the messes of life.

In the name of your powerful Son, Jesus, amen.

41

I commend you to God and to the word of His grace, which is able to build you up and give you an inheritance among all those who are sanctified.

ACTS 20:32

Dear Father God, I praise you for who you are. You are generous and compassionate to your children.

Some days I feel lost and unsure. Help me go to your Word and understand its truth. Use your Word to build me up and strengthen me every day.

Prompt my friends to read your Word and to commit it to memory so they will always have access to your promises. Give them a desire to study the Bible together and to strengthen one another with your instructions.

Thank you for the Bible. Thank you for the friendships that encourage me to be a student of the Word and to be committed to you.

In the powerful name of Jesus, amen.

42

Plans go wrong for lack of advice;
many advisers bring success.

PROVERBS 15:22 NLT

Father God, I praise you for who you are and what you mean to me. You are so good in all your ways, and your Word tells me that you are my wonderful Counselor.

I ask you for wisdom today. Let it flow out of me and into my friendships. Help me not only to seek wise counsel but also to heed it.

Please guide my friends on their journeys today. Help them seek you always. Let their paths be made straight and sure.

Thank you for being a constant presence in my life. Your advice is trustworthy, and I can rest in it, realizing you want the best for me. I am grateful for friends who encourage me with your wisdom and truth.

In your Son's name I pray, amen.

43

Two people are better off than one, for they can help each other succeed. If one person falls, the other can reach out and help. But someone who falls alone is in real trouble.

ECCLESIASTES 4:9-10 NLT

Gracious Father, every good and perfect gift comes from you, especially the friendships you've given me. I praise you for your attention to every detail of my life, including relationships.

I want to be strong for my friends when they go through trials and storms. Help me pick them up and point them toward you in every situation. Enable me to laugh with them as they rejoice and cry beside them as they struggle.

My friends have been such blessings to me. I ask that you give them strength for their days, whatever season they're in, and guard their steps. If they falter, don't let them fall.

Thank you for the gift of friendship. I'm so grateful for the joy and companionship my friends bring. You never fail to provide just what I need—like people who draw me closer to you.

In your gracious name, amen.

44

Ointment and perfume delight the heart,
And the sweetness of a man's friend
gives delight by hearty counsel.

PROVERBS 27:9

Dear Lord, your presence is like a sweet perfume drifting over my life. I praise you for your goodness and provision! You are worthy to be praised.

I ask you to prepare me today so I might be a sweet aroma for my friends. I want to bless them as they continually bless me. Help me to be aware of their needs and to focus on them, putting my own agenda aside.

Equip my friends today to rest in your presence, lingering there and being refreshed in you. Let them find their full delight in your love today.

Thank you for the sweetness of friendship. Laughter and late-night talks refresh my spirit and fill me with joy.

In Jesus' name, amen.

45

*Rejoice with those who rejoice, and
weep with those who weep.*

ROMANS 12:15

Father God, you know every hair on my head and every word before it leaves my mouth. My days were written out before I was born. I praise you for your deep knowledge of me. You know what makes me happy, what makes me sad, and what hurts me. You bottle my tears.

Help me not to be selfishly caught up in my own joys and sorrows but to be a friend who cries when my friends cry and who laughs when they laugh. Bonds are created through shared tears and laughter, and I want to be a good friend.

Be with them as they experience both joy and sorrow. When they're full of joy, let that passion bubble over and strengthen our friendship. When they hurt, let them feel your presence, and let them know I am here for them.

Thank you for the friends who laugh with me, celebrate with me, and encourage me. Thank you for those heart-to-heart talks that draw us closer to one another and to you.

In your Son's holy name, amen.

46

A person finds joy in giving an apt reply—
and how good is a timely word!

PROVERBS 15:23 NIV

D ear Lord God, you are the giver of words. I praise you for that gift. You blessed me with the ability to speak to my friends' hearts.

May I always remember that a kind word spoken at the right time can bring hope to a friend with a broken heart. Tame my tongue so I will speak only encouraging words.

Help my friends use their words wisely and carefully. When they're tempted to spout off in fear, doubt, or anger, remind them to be gentle. Guide their words so they will spread joy.

Thank you for friends who lift me up, encourage me, and speak your truth into my life. Thank you for providing me with so many loved ones who use their words to heal and not to hurt. I'm very grateful for them.

In the name of Jesus Christ, amen.

47

We took sweet counsel together,
And walked to the house of God in the throng.

PSALM 55:14

Heavenly Father, I love going to church to worship you, to learn more about your character, and to fellowship with other believers. You have provided me a community of believers where I can grow in your grace.

Let me be a sweet encouragement to my friends at church to draw closer to you. Help me be free with my worship so they might also have the courage to express themselves freely.

Help my friends attend church faithfully and grow alongside me as we worship you together. Stretch and develop their faith as they learn more about you.

I love learning about you through fellowship with my friends. Thank you for that opportunity and for the friendships you've given me in my church. It's such a gift to worship beside them.

In your sweet name, amen.

48

When my father and my mother forsake me,
Then the Lord will take care of me.

PSALM 27:10

Almighty God, you are a constant in my life. I praise you for your faithfulness. Even if everyone around me fails, you never do. I can always count on your presence.

Equip me to trust you in new ways and to greater depths. Help me release any fears I'm carrying, and remind me that you have never left me and will never forsake me. In turn, I want to be someone my friends can trust and depend on at all times.

Bless my friends with your presence when they struggle with loneliness. Be the companion they seek. Pursue their hearts, and reassure them that they are never alone because you are always there.

Thank you for the gift of your constant presence. Thank you for the joy of friendship and the companionship it brings.

In the powerful name of Jesus, amen.

49

A friend loves at all times,
And a brother is born for adversity.

PROVERBS 17:17

Heavenly Father, you are the very definition of love. I praise you for the many ways you show your love for me—through music, through your creation, and through the people you've placed in my life.

Help me reflect that love to others, especially my friends. Provide opportunities for me to be there for them in good times and bad and to encourage them through hugs, small gestures of kindness, and messages of hope, as they have done for me.

Strengthen my friends for whatever they're facing. Help them shine your love into all circumstances—even when doing so is hard or messy. Give them everything they need today, and provide them with an extra measure of grace.

Thank you for the blessing of friendships saturated in your love. I'm so grateful we don't have to navigate life on our own.

In Jesus' name, amen.

50

And Jesus spoke to them, saying, ". . . Go therefore
and make disciples of all the nations, baptizing
them in the name of the Father and of the Son and
of the Holy Spirit, teaching them to observe all
things that I have commanded you; and lo, I am
with you always, even to the end of the age."

MATTHEW 28:18–20

Heavenly Father, I praise you for the opportunities we have to spread the good news of the gospel. You are so loving, and you desire that everyone in the world would hear about your Son, Jesus.

Help me to partner with my friends in spreading the word about salvation and to speak about my faith plainly and simply. Prompt me to follow through when I hesitate to share your love with those I meet.

Give my friends courage as they seek to share your love with those who haven't heard of you. Provide them clarity as they talk about you, and inspire them to be strong witnesses motivated by love for your children.

Thank you for the opportunity to stand alongside my friends as we tell others about your grace.

In Jesus' name, amen.

51

Those who wait on the LORD
Shall renew their strength;
They shall mount up with wings like eagles,
They shall run and not be weary,
They shall walk and not faint.

ISAIAH 40:31

God of wonders, I praise you for who you are and how you take care of me. You always provide me with strength when I'm weak and perseverance when I feel as if I can't continue. You are so good to me.

Give me strong legs and determination as I run this race. Keep me moving forward even when the trail is bumpy and unsure. Lengthen my strides of faith, and prepare me to carry on when I'm scared or when all seems lost.

Help my friends find their strength in you during their rocky times. Let them spread their wings and fly despite adversity. Renew their energy daily, and give them your peace and comfort when they're struggling to keep going.

I am so grateful for the friends who run beside me and help me persevere.

In the precious name of Jesus, amen.

52

Fear not, for I am with you;
Be not dismayed, for I am your God.
I will strengthen you,
Yes, I will help you,
I will uphold you with My righteous right hand.

ISAIAH 41:10

Heavenly Father, I praise you for your protection. Fear is a real battle, yet you tell me that perfect love casts out fear.

It is easy for me to fall into the trap of fear. Teach me to trust in you. You are my strength and my portion, and I have no reason to be afraid. But in those moments when fear seems inevitable, equip me with a clear perspective, and remind me that I won't have to face it alone.

Be with my friends and help them find courage in the midst of their fears. Enable them to fight depression and discouragement through your strength.

Thank you for being my hero and my protector. You're my safety net in an unsafe world, and I am so grateful you are always for me. Thank you for friends who encourage me to trust you.

In the name of Jesus, amen.

53

The LORD shall preserve you from all evil;
He shall preserve your soul.
The LORD shall preserve your going out and your coming in
From this time forth, and even forevermore.

PSALM 121:7-8

Dear Lord, this world is so uncertain. Yet you are good in the midst of the evil. I praise you for your love and protection.

When the world gets especially dark, help me trust you and look for your light and not be afraid of the shadows. I want always to remember how close you are to me. You're my refuge. Help me encourage my friends and those around me with that truth.

When my friends face trials—sickness, broken relationships, or financial struggles—remind them you are in control. Please protect my friends and keep them safe. Guard their steps and all their ways.

Thank you for your protection, for being a strong tower when we feel like everything is crumbling around us.

In the name of Jesus, amen.

54

My intercessor is my friend
as my eyes pour out tears to God.

JOB 16:20 NIV

Lord Jesus, I praise you for your strength and protection. When I think about how strong you are compared to how weak I am, I'm overwhelmed. You alone are worthy of praise.

Remind me to focus on how big you are instead of how big my problems are. Remind me that you are my strong fortress and are always there for me to run to when life gets hard. I want to rest in your protection and not stress over things I can't control.

Peace and rest come from you. Remind my friends of that when they're too weary to carry on.

Thank you for loving and protecting me. You are my help when I'm in trouble, and I'm grateful I don't have to navigate life alone. You are always with me, and you've given me friends who walk beside me through life's valleys.

In the name of Jesus Christ, amen.

55

So we may boldly say: "The LORD is my helper;
I will not fear. What can man do to me?"

HEBREWS 13:6

Prince of Peace, it's easy for me to be overwhelmed by the world. When I turn on the news, the headlines often cast fear over my day. But in the midst of that, I praise you because you are still in control.

Remind me who runs the universe. Remind me who sits on the throne. Let me not fear people or their evil plans. Instead, I want to hold tightly to the truth that nothing takes you by surprise.

Please protect my friends and give them confidence in you and your strength. Remind them that they don't have to be afraid but can boldly trust you, regardless of what's happening in their cities or workplaces or schools.

Thank you for watching over my friends and me. Thank you for friends who take care of me in hard times. I'm grateful for heart-to-heart conversations with them when the world seems darkest.

In the holy name of Jesus, amen.

56

Many people claim to be loyal,
but it is hard to find a trustworthy person.
PROVERBS 20:6 NCV

Father God, you are trustworthy. You are the only one who never fails and never breaks a promise. You are worthy of my trust. And because I can trust you, I submit to you.

I want to live in a way that shows how much I trust you. I want to submit to you instead of making my own plans.

Help my friends see that trusting you is always best. It is tempting at times to go against your will or your plan, but that always leads to heartache and disaster. Protect my friends from rebelling against you, and give them soft hearts that will be swayed toward you and away from the evil that seeks to devour them.

Thank you for your Word and its instructions for handling moments of weakness and temptation. Thank you for being worthy of my trust. I'm so grateful for friends who remind me that your plan is always best.

In Jesus' name I pray, amen.

57

As iron sharpens iron,
so a friend sharpens a friend.

PROVERBS 27:17 NLT

Heavenly Father, you are so good to your children. I love how you use little things in my day to shed light on what you're doing behind the scenes. You are worthy to be praised.

When iron rubs against iron, it grows sharper and becomes more effective. Help me sharpen my friends. I want to help prepare them for your purposes and your kingdom. I want to be a quality tool in your hands.

Sometimes being sharpened can be uncomfortable or even downright painful. Please give my friends grace during those difficult times. Help them develop and grow in grace and truth.

Thank you for giving me friends who make me a better person, friends who help me stay sharp and focused on what matters most.

In the name of your holy Son, amen.

58

Open rebuke is better
Than love carefully concealed.
Faithful are the wounds of a friend,
But the kisses of an enemy are deceitful.

PROVERBS 27:5–6

Lord God, I know you discipline us because you love us. Thank you for showing your heart for your children this way. You've sent friends into my life to guide me along my journey, and they are priceless gifts to me.

When my friends give me wise counsel, help me receive it with a willing heart. Help me not shy away from their correction and instruction. Thank you for friends who love me enough to tell the truth even when it's hard for me to hear.

And please help my friends receive wisdom from me. Strengthen our friendships with hearts that always want the best for one another.

In your Son's name, amen.

59

Now we exhort you, brethren, warn those
who are unruly, comfort the fainthearted,
uphold the weak, be patient with all.

1 THESSALONIANS 5:14

Father, I praise you for your patience toward your people. You've blessed me in so many ways despite my impatience.

I want to trust your timing and not try to work things out on my own. When my friends are struggling to be patient, help me be there for them and guide them to trust your Word and your timing.

Help me embrace your comfort and strength so I can pass it on to those I love. My friends need your comfort, patience, and guidance. Let them find all they need in you, and equip them to be vessels of comfort, patience, and wisdom to others. Remind them that whatever problem they have, it is not too big for us to solve together with your guidance.

Thank you for being an example of love, comfort, and patience. I'm so grateful for my friends who show me how important those traits are and who inspire me to be better.

In the name of Jesus, amen.

60

A troublemaker plants seeds of strife;
gossip separates the best of friends.

PROVERBS 16:28 NLT

Great God, you are so good to me. Healthy friendships are a gift from you, but the Enemy wants to separate those friendships with strife.

I ask that you sow peace in my relationships. When gossip tries to divide us, give me discernment to see the Enemy's trick and to stop it with a gentle response. I want always to speak of my friends as the treasures they are and never tear them down.

Help my friends recognize the severity of gossip in their lives. I ask that you protect our friendships from unkind words, rumors, and malicious talk. Let the words of our mouths glorify and honor you.

Thank you for the kind words my friends say to me. They build me up with their compassion and encouragement, which I know is a gift from you.

In Christ's name, amen.

61

A hot-tempered person stirs up conflict,
but the one who is patient calms a quarrel.

PROVERBS 15:18 NIV

D ear heavenly Father, Jesus is the ultimate example of peace in the face of persecution. He didn't defend himself or grow angry when tormented on the cross. Rather, he asked forgiveness for his persecutors.

Help me to do the same. Instead of being angry, I want to follow the example of Jesus and pray for those who injure me. I want to be like Jesus and be slow to anger, especially with my friends and those I love the most.

Some of my friends struggle with their tempers. Help them hold their tongues when they're tempted to give a hurtful response. Help them remember Jesus' example.

Thank you for giving us the ability to choose peace over anger. Thank you that we don't have to give in to our natural desires.

I'm so grateful my friends understand me and love me even when I'm not at my best.

In the name of your precious Son, amen.

62

"Let each one of you speak truth with his neighbor,"
for we are members of one another. "Be angry,
and do not sin": do not let the sun go down on
your wrath, nor give place to the devil.

EPHESIANS 4:25–27

F ather God, I praise you because you are honest. You cannot lie, and you despise lying tongues.

I want to follow your example in this. I want to speak the truth always and in love. Help me resist the urge to lie when I'm caught doing something I shouldn't do. And I don't want to be guilty of lies of omission or lies to protect feelings.

When my friends are tempted to lie, give them the courage to be honest. Please guard our friendships, and let them always be built on truth, because we love one another and understand that lying never helps the situation.

Thank you for being an example of truth. I am so grateful I have friends who aren't afraid to tell me the truth.

In your Son's name, amen.

63

Pursue peace with all people, and holiness,
without which no one will see the Lord: looking
carefully lest anyone fall short of the grace of
God; lest any root of bitterness springing up cause
trouble, and by this many become defiled.

HEBREWS 12:14-15

Almighty God, I praise you for your heart for peace. Just as parents long for their children to love one another and get along, you desire for your people to live in peace with one another.

Help me not to harbor bitterness or unforgiveness toward my family or friends but to be an example of peacekeeping and holiness.

Be with my friends when they struggle with bitterness and unforgiveness. Help them let go of grudges and seek you instead of revenge. Remind them to pursue peace in all their relationships and not to give way to anger.

Thank you for friends who are comfortable telling me when they're angry with me so we can work things out. Thank you for your love for us and for your incredible blessings on our friendships.

In the holy name of Jesus, amen.

64

Therefore, as God's chosen people, holy and
dearly loved, clothe yourselves with compassion,
kindness, humility, gentleness and patience.

COLOSSIANS 3:12 NIV

Heavenly Father, you are so patient with me. I praise you for your patience toward me, for always bearing with me in love. You alone give peace that passes understanding.

Give me the grace to show that same love to my friends. Help me to be patient with them when we disagree and to demonstrate your gentleness and humility when my instinct is to demand my own way and my own opinion.

Help my friends embrace patience and peace. When we struggle to get along, give us the tools to work out our problems so we can show your love to others.

Thank you for calling me yours. Thank you for friends who understand that life can get hard and tempers can be short, but love between real friends lasts forever because of your blessing.

In your Son's name, amen.

65

*The Spirit Himself bears witness with our spirit that we
are children of God, and if children, then heirs—heirs
of God and joint heirs with Christ, if indeed we suffer
with Him, that we may also be glorified together.*

ROMANS 8:16–17

Heavenly Father, I praise you for your goodness and
consistency toward your children. I don't deserve
it, but you have made me an heir with Jesus because of
your great love.

Help me today to remember my place. When I feel
broken down and beat up, remind me I am a child of
God. When truth feels like a lie, help me not to doubt but
to cling to your promises.

Remind my friends of their standing with you.
When they struggle, whisper their names and reassure
them that all the hardships will be worth it one day. Help
them see that this life is temporary, but the eternal glory
waiting for them will outweigh the bad times.

Thank you for calling us your children when we
should be servants.

In the name of the Most High King, Jesus, amen.

66

Come now, you who say, "Today or tomorrow
we will go to such and such a city, spend a year
there, buy and sell, and make a profit"; whereas
you do not know what will happen tomorrow.

JAMES 4:13–14

Dear Lord, I praise you. Nothing slips through your hands. You are a God of organization and detail. You know it all, and you know what's best.

I often make plans and am disappointed when those plans fail. Help me trust in your plans and not in my own. Give me a desire to come to you first thing every morning and ask what you want me to do with my day.

Help my friends surrender their days to you. Help them see that you are directing their steps and that you are the best choreographer they could ask for. Remind them of your deep love for them and your attention to the details of their lives.

Thank you for watching over my friends and me. Thank you for always being right on time.

In the precious name of your Son, Jesus, amen.

67

Do not forget my law,
But let your heart keep my commands;
For length of days and long life
And peace they will add to you.

PROVERBS 3:1–2

Father God, I praise you for your laws. Because of my rebellious nature, I don't always keep your commands. But your laws are good, and they are for my good.

Help me never to dismiss your commands. I want to be obedient to your Word. I know that when I am, I will experience joy and wellness of soul. Strengthen me to live out that desire to please you.

Be with my friends when they're tempted to sin against you. Remind them that keeping your law isn't just a good idea but is life and peace. Show them how they will thrive and flourish when they follow you and obey you.

Thank you for your laws. Your instructions always guide me to what's best. Your laws protect me from myself.

In the sweet name of Jesus, amen.

68

Depend on the LORD in whatever you do,
and your plans will succeed.

PROVERBS 16:3 NCV

D ear Father God, I praise you for your plan for my life. You are the God of the entire universe, yet you are so good to me and are involved in the details of my day.

Help me trust you with my day and every detail in it so I will walk with you and not go down my own path. I want my steps to be ordered by you so my mind will be at ease.

Help my friends trust that you are at work in their lives too. I pray that they will strive to honor you with every part of their days. As they commit their steps to you, give them peace and sureness of mind. Provide them with clarity so they don't have to wander aimlessly but instead will live with purpose.

Thank you for giving me friends who walk with me on this path through life. I look forward to every celebration and joyous moment to be shared.

In Jesus' name, amen.

69

And my God will meet all your needs according
to the riches of his glory in Christ Jesus.

PHILIPPIANS 4:19 NIV

Dear heavenly Father, you are the keeper of a thousand cattle on a thousand hills. You graciously provide for all your children's needs. I praise you for your provision!

I need to be reminded of this when I get discouraged about my finances. Help me not to stress over the balance in my bank account but to remember that you own it all and will take care of me.

Remind my friends that they can be confident of your provision. Keep them from feeling hopeless when bills pile up or the collectors call. Equip them to trust you even when it seems there is no way out of the situation.

Thank you for providing in your timing. I never have to doubt or worry if you're going to come through for me. Even when things don't make sense in the moment, I know you have a good plan.

In the name of your Son, amen.

70

Don't be concerned for your own good
but for the good of others.

1 CORINTHIANS 10:24 NLT

Dear God in heaven, I praise you for who you are and for the examples you give us in your Word. You sent Jesus to us as a perfect example of selflessness and heavenly love on earth.

It's easy to get caught up in my personal struggles and forget to put others first. Rid my heart of selfishness, and equip me to put my friends' interests before my own. Don't allow me to forget to minister to others in their struggles.

Bless and strengthen my friends. Give them an extra measure of your love, peace, and joy in the midst of their trials. Help us bless one another with acts of service and kindness.

Thank you that, through the work of the Holy Spirit, you make possible what seems impossible: being selfless.

In your name I pray, amen.

71

A man who has friends must himself be friendly,
But there is a friend who sticks closer than a brother.

PROVERBS 18:24

Abba Father, you are good to your children. There are many who no longer have their earthly parents, and you fill that role with your love. I praise you for the way you care specifically for each of your children.

I want to be the kind of friend who is closer than a brother. Help me meet the needs of those friends you've entrusted to me by being there for them completely and purely. Help me be the sibling they might feel they're missing in their lives.

I pray that my friends will sense your deep love for them. If they don't have earthly families, remind them of your provision and care. Let them embrace you as their Father.

Sometimes family isn't born but chosen. Thank you for the friendships that mean as much to me as family does.

In Jesus' name, amen.

72

*Love is patient, love is kind. It does not envy, it
does not boast, it is not proud. It does not dishonor
others, it is not self-seeking, it is not easily angered,
it keeps no record of wrongs. Love does not delight
in evil but rejoices with the truth. It always protects,
always trusts, always hopes, always perseveres.*

1 CORINTHIANS 13:4-7 NIV

Dear Jesus, you were and always will remain the ultimate example of true love. I praise you for your love for me even when I am so unlovable.

I want to love purely and simply. I want to rejoice with my friends when they're happy, believe in them when they falter, and always hope for the best for them. Equip me to do this in your strength.

Help my friends find true love in you. Help them align their hearts with yours and be filled with love so they can pour it out on others. And help me reflect your love.

Thank you that your love never runs out. Thank you that I have friends who show me love every day, whether it's through a timely text message, a funny social-media post, or a big hug.

In your precious name, amen.

73

If you bring your gift to the altar, and there remember that your brother has something against you, leave your gift there before the altar, and go your way. First be reconciled to your brother, and then come and offer your gift.

MATTHEW 5:23-24

Dear God in heaven, I praise you for your forgiving heart. You are the God of not only the second chance but also the third and fourth and fiftieth. Even though I don't deserve it, your love covers me, and your forgiveness washes me white as snow.

I don't want to hold grudges against strangers, family members, or my best friends. Show me how to forgive freely.

Help my friends forgive easily. When I hurt them, help them forgive me. When others speak harsh words or wrong them, remind my friends that forgiveness is the key to true freedom.

Thank you for being an example of forgiveness. When I feel it's too hard to forgive someone, I only have to think of your sacrifice to realize it is possible through you.

In the name of Jesus, amen.

74

For where two or three are gathered together in
My name, I am there in the midst of them.

MATTHEW 18:20

Dear Jesus, you are sufficient. You are all we need in this life. Yet you also bless us with friendships and human love. I praise you for providing community and fellowship.

Remind me that there is power in numbers. Help me not withdraw when I feel discouraged; instead, prompt me to be vulnerable and open with my friends and invite them into my hurt or pain. Your Word promises that when we pray together, things happen!

Remind my friends that they are never alone. Help them to be bold in admitting their need for you and for others. And help them to freely ask for prayer.

Thank you for never leaving me alone, and thank you for loving me through my friends. Because of them, I often feel your presence in new ways.

In your name I pray, amen.

75

*A person's friends should be kind to
him when he is in trouble.*

JOB 6:14 NCV

Dear heavenly Father, I praise you for your attention to me when I go through painful times. You never leave me but continue to show your great love for me in the darkest days.

When life is sunny, remind me that my friends may be struggling with shadows. Don't let me be so caught up in my own life that I forget to pray for and care for them.

Encourage my friends today in the midst of their hardships and trials. Help them show others the kind of friendship they want to receive. Remind them to be kind in all their relationships and not be just fair-weather friends.

Thank you for friends who meet my needs, for friends who celebrate with me over job promotions and new relationships, and for friends who mourn with me when I go through layoffs or breakups.

In the name of Jesus, amen.

76

Two are better than one,
Because they have a good reward for their labor.
For if they fall, one will lift up his companion.

ECCLESIASTES 4:9–10

Father, you did not create us to be alone. You are with me. The Holy Spirit is with me, and you have blessed me in so many ways.

But today I feel lonely. I feel lost, and I want friends I can depend on to help me when I fall. Please bring people like that into my life.

Show me the people around me, who are also lonely, that I could befriend. Give them the hope and godly confidence they need to meet new people.

Thank you for always hearing my prayers.

In Jesus' name, amen.

77

Be kind to one another, tenderhearted,
forgiving one another,
even as God in Christ forgave you.

EPHESIANS 4:32

Dear heavenly Father, you are so good to me. You forgive me, love me, and are kind to me. You are the perfect example of how to love others when it can be hard.

Some days it seems easier to hold a grudge and be upset than to offer forgiveness or be tenderhearted toward my friends. Remind me that I don't deserve forgiveness but, because of Christ, I have it anyway.

Help my friends have forgiving hearts when I hurt them. Prompt them to be tenderhearted toward me and to remember that gentle answers turn away anger but harsh words escalate the situation.

Thank you for providing me with friends who see the best in me even when I don't see it myself. Thank you for friends who are willing to forgive because they have been forgiven first by you. What a gift they are to me.

In the sweet name of Jesus, amen.

PRAYERS *for* GRACE AND FORGIVENESS

78

In the multitude of words sin is not lacking,
But he who restrains his lips is wise.

PROVERBS 10:19

Heavenly Father, you are holy. You are untainted and perfect.

Sometimes I talk too much and say things I later regret. Sometimes, I confess, I listen to gossip when I should walk away. When I am tempted to say more than I should, including hurtful chatter, prompt me to keep quiet. Help me speak only words of compassion and love, words that uplift and glorify you.

When gossip threatens the relationships of the people around me, erase it with kindness and close every mouth. Help everyone focus on the work, building up rather than tearing down one another. Keep our words few, and multiply our accomplishments.

Thank you for language so we can express our joy and love for you.

In your name, amen.

79

All Scripture is given by inspiration of God, and is profitable for doctrine, for reproof, for correction, for instruction in righteousness, that the man of God may be complete, thoroughly equipped for every good work.

2 TIMOTHY 3:16–17

Gracious heavenly Father, you breathed life into the world. Your presence surrounds me, and your Word stands forever.

When I'm challenged, help me remember that the truth of your Word is the guideline I should use for living a life that pleases you. Help me grow stronger and wiser in the time I spend with you.

Thank you for your unchanging Word. Thank you that I can use it as my guideline for daily living. Knowing that my faith and life are grounded in your truth gives me the strength to extend grace and forgiveness.

In your glorious and holy name, amen.

80

"The eyes of the LORD are on the righteous, and His ears are open to their prayers; but the face of the LORD is against those who do evil." And who is he who will harm you if you become followers of what is good? But even if you should suffer for righteousness' sake, you are blessed.

1 PETER 3:12–14

Father in heaven, you are the ultimate judge of righteousness. Your ways are holy and fair.

I work hard, Lord, and sometimes I don't feel that I get any recognition. Sometimes I'm criticized for making the right choices in a world that no longer values honesty. When these things happen, remind me that your love and recognition are more valuable than any earthly acknowledgments.

When others would rather be popular than do what is right, convict their hearts. Bring them back to your truth.

Thank you for your mercy when we fail, Lord. Thank you for your strength and love when we feel persecuted. Most of all, thank you for letting us work for your kingdom.

In your blessed name, amen.

81

Therefore, having been justified by faith, we have peace with God through our Lord Jesus Christ, through whom also we have access by faith into this grace in which we stand, and rejoice in hope of the glory of God.

ROMANS 5:1-2

Lord, your holiness is untainted. We cannot fathom the beauty of your greatness and grace.

I'm never going to be perfect, God, but I want to be an example of your kingdom in every moment of my life. In situations where I can't expressly say your name, let my actions speak louder than words ever could.

I pray that the Holy Spirit will prompt the hearts of the people around me to want to know you more. Help them recognize that "something different" in me—your peace and your presence.

Thank you for saving my soul so I might be your witness. Thank you for filling my life with friends and family. I know you put every one of them there for a reason.

In Christ's name, amen.

82

*For all have sinned and fall short of the glory of
God, being justified freely by His grace through
the redemption that is in Christ Jesus.*

ROMANS 3:23-24

Dear God, your love is unending and never failing,
and your grace is a constant gift.

Some days I don't feel deserving of the privilege of
having a family. I forget things. I lose my patience. I
neglect the ones I love the most. But I know I am made
complete through your sacrifice.

Be with my loved ones today, Father. I pray that we
will extend grace to one another so that we will function
as a team with you at the center.

Thank you for grace—the greatest gift of all—and
the way it appears in my life. When I witness moments
of grace, I'm refreshed and renewed.

In your name I pray, amen.

83

For by grace you have been saved through faith,
and that not of yourselves; it is the gift of God,
not of works, lest anyone should boast.

EPHESIANS 2:8-9

Father, you alone can save. There is no one like you. You have redeemed the world.

Today I feel inadequate. I feel guilty for not doing more for my family and friends. Remind me that I am enough because it is not me but Christ in me who makes me worthy.

Protect my loved ones when I can't be there for them. Surround my loved ones with the kind of unconditional love only you can give.

Thank you that you are enough for me and that your grace will always be sufficient.

In Jesus' name, amen.

84

Whoever desires to become great among you, let him be your servant. And whoever desires to be first among you, let him be your slave—just as the Son of Man did not come to be served, but to serve, and to give His life a ransom for many.

MATTHEW 20:26-28

Jesus, you saved us from our sins even though we didn't deserve your sacrifice. Glorious is your name!

In some areas of my life, I'm in a position of leadership, and I ask you to remind me of your example. You were the greatest leader of all mankind, yet you came to serve. Let me be a servant to those I'm leading so their lives may be even more rewarding.

Help those in my circle extend support to the leadership in our community even when they don't understand difficult decisions that are made. Prompt them to agree with the common cause—the greater good.

Thank you for those with whom I work. Thank you for those I lead. Help me follow your example as I serve them.

In your name, amen.

85

Are not five sparrows sold for two copper coins?
And not one of them is forgotten
before God. But the very hairs of
your head are all numbered. Do
not fear therefore; you are of more
value than many sparrows.

LUKE 12:6-7

Dear Father, you know each of your children by name. Nothing escapes your gaze.

There are days when I feel overlooked by my friends and family. I feel underappreciated, as if they don't notice all the things I do for them each day. Remind me that your love is all I need. I am worthy simply because you created me.

I pray for other people who feel this way and for my friends who have forgotten who they are in you. May they feel loved and cherished.

Thank you for providing all the love and affirmation I need.

In Jesus' name, amen.

86

Not by works of righteousness which we have
done, but according to His mercy He saved us.

TITUS 3:5

God, you are worthy of our praise and our gratitude. With everything in me, I praise you.

On days when I feel that I am at the end of myself, remind me that I don't need to be perfect. When I strive for perfection, I fall short. When I rely on you instead of myself, I see how great you are. Teach me to focus on you.

Be with my loved ones today. Teach them to rely on you. Give them exactly what they need to get through today.

Thank you for reminding me to rest in your promise of grace.

In Christ's name, amen.

87

Accept one another, then, just as Christ accepted
you, in order to bring praise to God.

ROMANS 15:7 NIV

Father, you are the creator of all. You knew me before I was born, and you know me intimately still.

My identity is so wrapped up in my job that when I make a mistake, I feel as if I am a failure as a person. But you know every part of me and still accept me. Remind me of this throughout my day.

May my friends and family know that they are loved not only by me but by you. May they find their worth in you and not in what others say about them.

Thank you for my friends and family and loving them even more than I do. Thank you for the simple joys and the extravagant love that abound. Thank you for surrounding me with such amazing people.

In Jesus' name, amen.

PRAYERS *for* GUIDANCE

88

*Put on the whole armor of God, that you may be
able to stand against the wiles of the devil.*

EPHESIANS 6:11

Heavenly Father, your power knows no limits. Your enemies tremble at the mere thought of you. You are my God and my Savior, and my hope is in you all day long.

I need every piece of your armor to protect me, Lord. I know the evil I fight starts in the spiritual kingdom. Please give me your spiritual protection. Prepare me to face all my challenges, both physical and spiritual.

Thank you for protecting and guiding my family and me. I am so grateful you have prepared me with your Word for whatever is to come.

In your name, amen.

89

God is our refuge and strength,
A very present help in trouble.

PSALM 46:1

God, you are the origin of all that is good, righteous, and true. You are high above all nations and all peoples. You are a sanctuary for those who call on your name.

I confess that there are days I feel my spirit and resolve weaken. I have so much pressure from my job and the expectations of serving others. I desperately need your strength to uphold me and renew my spirit. Please remind me to be anxious for nothing because you are near. Lead me through this tough period.

Protect my family today. Shield them from trouble and the worries of the world. Teach them to rest in your promises so they will have peace.

I am extremely grateful for your gentle spirit, which can calm the raging seas around us. Thank you for your unfailing love, support, and guidance.

In Jesus' name, amen.

90

"Because he loves me," says the LORD, *"I will rescue him;*
I will protect him, for he acknowledges my name."

PSALM 91:14 NIV

Heavenly Father, you are compassionate and patient with your people. You redeem and guard your own. Your mercies are new every day.

Please protect me in all aspects of my life—my job, my family, my spiritual walk, and other areas. Direct my prayer life, and continue to teach me to follow you better. Help me acknowledge you in everything I do, and let me rest in your divine protection.

Strengthen my friends and family. Their concerns may be different than mine but are just as important and worrisome for them. Teach them to continually praise you and your name regardless of what they face. May they walk through their days with a bold confidence that you are guiding and watching over them.

Thank you for revealing yourself to us. I am so grateful that you chose to save me and that you continually look after me.

In your Son's name, amen.

91

I will call upon the LORD, who is worthy to be praised;
So shall I be saved from my enemies.

2 SAMUEL 22:4

My father, you know every breath I will take and the length of my days. You order my every step. You alone are my God and my Savior.

Help me resist the temptations of the Evil One. The unseen Enemy is warring for my soul. Don't let me follow his plans, and protect me from my own foolish and, at times, wayward heart as well. Teach me to rely on you to keep my greatest adversary at bay.

Place a special protection around those who serve you. Let them see your divine shield all around them. Be their guide and their guardian.

I am so grateful that you watch over me and keep me focused on you. Thank you for giving us wisdom on how to face our challenges.

In your holy name, amen.

*Come to Me, all you who labor and are heavy
laden, and I will give you rest. Take My yoke upon
you and learn from Me, for I am gentle and lowly
in heart, and you will find rest for your souls.
For My yoke is easy and My burden is light.*

MATTHEW 11:28-30

Dear God, you hold the entire world in your hands. There is no limit to your strength and power.

Be with me when I feel the weight of my loved ones' struggles. Lift that burden from my shoulders.

And lift that burden from them too. Give my loved ones strength to face the difficult times and hope even when the darkness feels overwhelming.

I'm especially thankful for the wisdom of elders who have walked this path before me. Their insights help point me to you in every circumstance. Thank you for placing mentors in my life who lift me up.

In your powerful name I pray, amen.

93

He went a little farther, and fell on the ground, and
prayed that if it were possible, the hour might pass
from Him. And He said, "Abba, Father, all things
are possible for You. Take this cup away from Me;
nevertheless, not what I will, but what You will."

MARK 14:35-36

God, you love us so much that you did not spare even your own Son. The depth and scope of your love are unimaginable.

Jesus, help me strive to be obedient and to trust God just as you did when you set the supreme example. Work in my spirit so I will desire to follow the will of God wherever it leads, no matter how hard it might be. Teach me the humility and love I need to serve my God like this. I want my will to conform to your will.

Fill my friends and family with your love and mercy today. Renew their hearts with a deep appreciation for what you have done for them and for all of us.

Thank you for demonstrating true submission and reverence. I am grateful for the amazing work you did on the cross and are doing in my life.

In your holy name, amen.

94

*These things I have spoken to you, that in Me you may
have peace. In the world you will have tribulation;
but be of good cheer, I have overcome the world.*

JOHN 16:33

Father in heaven, you cast out all fear with your
perfect love. I am amazed by the perfect peace you
bring to me.

Today I am worried about my children. Temptations
surround them at school, with friends, online. Sometimes
I feel helpless. Give me wisdom, and help me release them
confidently to your care.

Protect my children today while they go about their
activities. Protect them from evil and temptation. Hold
them in your hands.

Thank you that even when I fear, I can trust in you.
Thank you that I can rest in you.

In Jesus' name, amen.

95

*You must not fear them, for the L*ORD
your God Himself fights for you.

DEUTERONOMY 3:22

F ather, I lift up your name and give you praise! You are the King whose greatness is unsearchable. You defend those you love.

I know you are in front of me in the battle. Give me the courage to face any trials and obstacles the Enemy throws my way. Quell my fears and concerns. Encourage me to remain strong in you and your plan for my life. Help me be fearless in the face of the adversary and his schemes.

Fight on behalf of my family. Wage war on whatever seeks to cause them harm or to place a wedge between you and them. Keep them safe and close to you.

Thank you for leading the way in my life and my career. I rejoice in knowing that you hate evil and will someday bring it to an end.

In Jesus' name, amen.

96

And who is he who will harm you if you become
followers of what is good? But even if you should
suffer for righteousness' sake, you are blessed.

1 PETER 3:13-14

F ather, no evil can defeat you. No problem is too big
for you. You see and know all.

Help me today, Lord. It is hard to let go of worry and
fear for my family. I am afraid of what could happen to
them. Give me peace when anxiety surfaces.

Keep the Evil One far from my loved ones today.
Do not let him take a single ounce of joy or happiness
from them.

Thank you for my suffering, for I know even in suffering that you are drawing me closer to you.

In Jesus' name, amen.

97

And Moses said to the people, "Do not be afraid.
Stand still, and see the salvation of the LORD,
which He will accomplish for you today."

EXODUS 14:13

God, you are a mighty warrior. You fight battles every day that I cannot see, and you are always victorious.

I need you to fight for me today. I feel weak, and I doubt when I know I should trust. I need faith that my family will be taken care of. The troubles we face seem so dark. Overcome my fear with your victory.

Fight for my family today, Father. When they feel sad or afraid or believe the problem is too big, show them how you will overcome.

Thank you that the battles belong to you, for you are capable and I am not.

In your name I pray this, amen.

98

The Lord is good, a stronghold in the day of trouble; and He knows those who trust in Him.

NAHUM 1:7

Father, you are good. You are righteous, and you are worthy.

Help me when I doubt your goodness. When I think about all the evil in the world, it makes me afraid for my loved ones. Teach me how to trust in your unfailing goodness.

Be a stronghold for my family in times of trouble. Lift them up, and teach them to depend on your strength and not their own.

Thank you for being a steady rock and strong foundation for each of us today.

In the name of Jesus, who is my refuge, amen.

99

But the Lord is faithful, who will establish
you and guard you from the evil one.

2 THESSALONIANS 3:3

My Father in heaven, you are the beginning and the end. You have gone before me and provided for me in all ways.

Lord, each year brings new challenges, and I can't always protect the ones I love. Release me from fear, and show me how to surrender them to you daily.

Be with my friends and family today. Be in their conversations and interactions with others.

Thank you for your faithfulness. You never leave us. You never forsake us.

In your name I pray, amen.

100

We are hard-pressed on every side, yet not crushed;
we are perplexed, but not in despair;
persecuted, but not forsaken;
struck down, but not destroyed.

2 CORINTHIANS 4:8–9

Dear God, you are bigger than my problems, worries, and fears. You are stronger than anything that could come against me or my family.

Give me strength today, Father. It feels as if everyone in my family is going through a hard time right now. Remind me that I am not forsaken and that you are on my side.

Remind my family of your promise that even when hard times come, they will not be destroyed. Even when they feel persecuted, you are with them.

Thank you that you walk beside me through every trial I face and have promised to bring me through them.

In Christ's name, amen.

PRAYERS *for* HEALING AND SAFETY

101

We should not trust in ourselves but in God
who raises the dead, who delivered us from
so great a death, and does deliver us; in
whom we trust that He will still deliver us.

CORINTHIANS 1:9–10

Father, you are the ultimate healer. Only you have the power to raise the dead to life and make all things new.

Help me trust my cares to you today. When my friend is sick, I feel helpless. Allow me to trust you with this burden.

Hear my prayer for healing my friend. Restore my loved one's energy today; increase our trust by giving us evidence of improvement.

Thank you for caring about our illnesses, no matter how minor they are. Father, knowing that you are embracing my friend brings us both comfort. Help me not forget this moment of healing prayer and your response to my pleas.

In Jesus' name, amen.

102

*Be strong and of good courage, do not fear
nor be afraid of them; for the LORD your
God, He is the One who goes with you. He
will not leave you nor forsake you.*

DEUTERONOMY 31:6

Dear heavenly Father, you never leave us, and you never forsake us. You are our protector and our deliverer. I praise you.

Give me strength and courage today. There is someone in my life who is sick. We don't know the diagnosis yet, and we are scared. Give us courage just for today.

One of my loved ones is trying to be strong for all of us right now. Please provide your rest and peace. Don't let any of us try to carry this burden alone.

Thank you for your promise to go with us and to go before us.

In Christ's name I pray, amen.

103

He was wounded for our transgressions,
He was bruised for our iniquities;
The chastisement for our peace was upon Him,
And by His stripes we are healed.

ISAIAH 53:5

Father, you sent your Son as a sacrifice for us. You are a good Father, who cares for your children more than we could ever know.

I feel burdened today. Watching my loved one suffer heavies my heart. Lift the burden from me, God, and give her rest from this illness.

Do not let my loved one's fear and pain prevent her from trusting you. She doesn't understand her suffering, but you do. I ask for quick healing and a full recovery.

Thank you that in the midst of even these difficult times, you bring moments of joy that I often take for granted.

It's in your name I pray, amen.

104

Heal me, O Lord, and I shall be healed;
Save me, and I shall be saved,
For You are my praise.

JEREMIAH 17:14

Father in heaven, you are good. There is no evil or impure thing in you. All good and perfect gifts come from you.

Remember me today. I need your saving grace and your healing. Fill me with it so that I can praise you.

I ask for healing for my family today. They need physical, spiritual, and emotional healing during this time in their lives. Be their comfort, Father.

Thank you for healing us ultimately by saving us. Thank you for the promise of eternity with you.

In Jesus' name, amen.

Now when the woman saw that she was not hidden, she came trembling; and falling down before Him, she declared to Him in the presence of all the people the reason she had touched Him and how she was healed immediately. And He said to her, "Daughter, be of good cheer; your faith has made you well. Go in peace."

LUKE 8:47-48

Dear Father, just one touch from you can heal the sick and make the blind see. You perform miracles every day.

Help me in my unbelief today. When I start to doubt your power and your ability to heal, remind me of the story of the woman who touched you and was healed immediately. Her faith made her well. Give me a faith like that.

I ask for healing for the sick children I know. Perform a miracle, God. We need a miracle. When everyone tells us there is no cure, give us hope that you are the cure.

Thank you for the gentle way that you deal with your children and all the ways that you provide.

In your name I pray, amen.

106

My son, give attention to my words;
Incline your ear to my sayings.
Do not let them depart from your eyes;
Keep them in the midst of your heart;
For they are life to those who find them,
And health to all their flesh.

PROVERBS 4:20-22

Dear God, your Word is good. It is life changing and life giving. It is steady and brings peace to all who listen.

Point me to scriptures today that are full of your promises. My heart aches for those who are sick and have been for so long. Bring me hope through your Word in a new way.

Comfort those who are ill. May they feel your arms around them as their bodies and hearts ache. Bring them healing, and allow them to rest well.

Thank you for giving us your Word so that we don't ever need to feel lost or alone.

In Jesus' name, amen.

107

O Lord my God, I cried out to You,
And You healed me.

PSALM 30:2

Good Father, you hear all our cries. You care deeply about each and every one of your children.

I ask for healing today. You say if we seek, we will find; if we cry out, you will heal. Heal my sick child. Bring him relief and renewed energy.

Be with my friends who are also experiencing illness. May their suffering draw them closer to you. Bring them miraculous healing.

I thank you for your mercy and faithfulness that never end. I thank you for friendships and the opportunity to support my friends. You've made us for community, and I am so grateful for the one you've given me.

In Christ's name I pray, amen.

PRAYERS *for*
HOME AND FAMILY

108

This is why a man leaves his father and mother and
unites with his wife, and they become one family.

GENESIS 2:24 NET

D ear Father, you can fix anything that is broken. Nothing and no one is unfixable for you. You are bigger than our pain and our problems.

Lord, it has been hard for me to get along with my parents and family in this phase of life. I feel independent, but they don't see me that way. Show me how to honor you and my parents.

Give my parents the courage to let go. When they are holding on to me and my siblings too much, replace their fear with peace, and comfort them during this time of change.

Thank you for giving us courage and strength.

In Jesus' name, amen.

109

The name of the LORD is a strong tower;
The righteous run to it and are safe.

PROVERBS 18:10

Dear Lord, you are the strong tower, the mighty fortress for your people. No one can stand against you.

Remind me to run to you daily. All too often I rely on my own strength and think I'm the only one who can protect my family and keep them from difficult situations. I can't. Only you can. Help me have the faith to trust you for our protection and care.

As my family walks through this day, they need the physical and spiritual protection only you can provide. Please be the strong tower for them and guide them so they will not try to rely on themselves but on you alone.

Thank you, Lord, for being my protector and shield in times of trouble.

In your precious name I pray, amen.

110

*I have been crucified with Christ; it is no longer I
who live, but Christ lives in me; and the life which
I now live in the flesh I live by faith in the Son of
God, who loved me and gave Himself for me.*

GALATIANS 2:20

Heavenly Father, you are gracious and merciful.
Only by your love and your Son's sacrifice on the
cross am I saved.

I need your help to fully understand this truth and
live it out in my life. I want to follow you and never forget or take for granted that you gave your Son's life for
mine. Each day help me to die a little more to the things
that keep me from a right relationship with you. Help me
walk in faith and set the example for my family.

Bless my family today. Help them live by faith and
set their eyes on you alone for their salvation. Guide my
children's hearts so they will walk with you every day.

Thank you for caring for me and my family and for
the precious gift of your Son.

In Jesus' holy name, amen.

111

He said, "Come." And when Peter had come down out of the boat, he walked on the water to go to Jesus. But when he saw that the wind was boisterous, he was afraid; and beginning to sink he cried out, saying, "Lord, save me!"

MATTHEW 14:29-30

Almighty God, you are in control of all things. Even the power of nature rests squarely in your hands.

Many times I am just like Peter. I start out with good intentions to follow you but quickly get frightened or discouraged, and my faith wavers. I want to follow you without faltering, with power and confidence in you and your plan for my life. Strengthen my faith. Please guide me so that when the storms of life come, I will keep my eyes and my heart focused on you, and I will not fear or doubt.

I ask you to be with my family through the storms of life, whether big or small. Teach them to look to you constantly and not to waver. Bless my home with the peace only you can bring.

Thank you for lifting us up in times of trouble and pain.

In your Son's name, amen.

112

*I know what it is to be in need, and I know what it
is to have plenty. I have learned the secret of being
content in any and every situation, whether well fed
or hungry, whether living in plenty or in want. I can
do all this through him who gives me strength.*

PHILIPPIANS 4:12–13 NIV

Father, you control our every circumstance, our every breath. Your power and majesty know no limits.

I confess that I struggle with contentment. I find myself complaining about one thing or another, desiring what I don't have instead of being grateful for what I do have. Please rid me of this attitude, and help me, instead, recognize the bounty of blessings you have given me.

Help me lead my family in achieving contentment, rather than chasing after the things culture says will provide fulfillment. Give each of us strength to resist the pull of the world. Guide our hearts and minds to find our satisfaction in you alone.

Thank you for quenching our spiritual thirst and comforting our souls.

In Christ's name, amen.

113

Love suffers long and is kind; love does not envy;
love does not parade itself, is not puffed up; does
not behave rudely, does not seek its own, is not
provoked, thinks no evil; does not rejoice in iniquity,
but rejoices in the truth; bears all things, believes
all things, hopes all things, endures all things.

1 CORINTHIANS 13:4-7

Lord, you are the perfect expression of love. Your love never ends, and your love never fails. Your love conquers all.

Help me understand what real love means and how to express that love to you and to the people in my life. Give me wisdom to know when to turn off the intensity that I need for my job and simply love the way you love. Help me serve, never forgetting to love as you teach us in your Word.

My desire is that our family will be filled with an abundance of love—true, godly love—for one another and for you. Please help us seek to love as you do.

Thank you for loving us first and bringing us into your family. Thank you for teaching us through your Son what love really is.

In Christ's name, amen.

114

They are no longer two but one flesh. Therefore what
God has joined together, let not man separate.

MATTHEW 19:6

Heavenly Father, no evil can stand against you. The schemes of the Enemy have no power in your awesome presence. You are a shield and a rock for your people.

Protect my marriage. Shield me against temptations that could threaten this marriage. Please pour out your love on us so our promises to each other and to you remain unbroken. Keep the Enemy from getting strongholds in our relationship. Help me use my words and actions to strengthen our bond and never harm it.

Bless, protect, encourage, and wrap your love around my spouse today. Help me and my spouse focus on our relationships with each other and with you.

Thank you for the gift of marriage. Thank you for giving me the strength to honor and cherish my spouse.

In your Son's name, amen.

115

Who can find a virtuous wife?
For her worth is far above rubies.
PROVERBS 31:10

Almighty Father, you are just and holy, the mighty God, the eternal one.

Help me appreciate my spouse more. My spouse provides so many blessings. I'm concerned that I don't give my life partner the love and respect I should. Please, Lord, grant me the heart to honor my partner. Help me be the spouse you want me to be.

Please guide my children today to appreciate their parents and surround them with love and encouragement. Lift my spouse's spirits.

Thank you for the wonderful spouse you have given me.

In Jesus' holy name, amen.

116

May the Lord watch between you and me
when we are absent one from another.

GENESIS 31:49

Father in heaven, your ways are not our ways, and your thoughts are so much higher than ours. Your wisdom is beyond anyone's understanding.

Life is full of challenges and ever-changing seasons: times of plenty, times of crisis, times of joy, and times of sorrow. But you are constant and steadfast in each season, whether joyful or challenging. Thank you for anchoring me and my family to the truth that is unshakable, in all seasons. You are a good and true Father, unwavering in your love and care.

Thank you, Jesus, for watching over us.

In your name I pray, amen.

117

In everything give thanks; for this is the
will of God in Christ Jesus for you.

1 THESSALONIANS 5:18

Dear God, by your mighty word you can move mountains and create life. And yet, in your magnificent glory you still know me by name and watch carefully over me and my family.

Father, thank you for everything you do. I owe my life and my every breath to you. I find it so easy to walk through my day and take for granted all the miracles and gifts in my life. Please forgive me. Change my heart and my attitude.

Give my family a spirit of thankfulness today. Help them see the multitude of reasons they have to thank you for this day you have made.

Thank you, Lord, for my life and my family. Thank you for joy, peace, and provision. Thank you that we can tell others about you. And thank you for loving us.

In Jesus' name, amen.

118

Do not worry, saying, "What shall we eat?" or "What shall we drink?" or "What shall we wear?" For after all these things the Gentiles seek. For your heavenly Father knows that you need all these things.

MATTHEW 6:31-32

My Father in heaven, you are the ultimate provider. You see the needs of your people and bless them mightily out of the abundance of your love.

I confess that I worry too often about how we will pay our bills, put food on the table, and prepare for the future. Help me trust in you as our provider and not stress out about the things of this world. Teach me to rely on you and your guidance for our provision and to appreciate the jobs you have given us so that we can earn a living.

Remind my family that you are their ultimate provider. As you meet their needs, may they give you the glory and honor for providing for them.

Thank you for taking such great care of us.

In your Son's name I pray, amen.

119

When you stand praying, if you hold anything
against anyone, forgive them, so that your
Father in heaven may forgive you your sins.

MARK 11:25 NIV

Lord God, you are the holy Redeemer. You have given us the perfect example of forgiveness and reconciliation in your Son, Jesus.

I have held on to many grudges and old grievances and hurts, Lord. I fear that they get in the way of my walk with you, but I struggle to forgive as you would have me do. I need your help. Please show me how to forgive and heal. Help me let go of the toxic attitudes that weigh down my heart and threaten my peace.

In my family, as in most, we've had conflicts and unresolved issues. Help us today to put aside past hurts and to reconcile. Heal us, Lord, and restore our relationships.

Thank you for showing us what forgiveness and reconciliation really look like. Thank you for healing our old wounds and helping us move forward.

In Jesus' name, amen.

120

I have come that they may have life, and that
they may have it more abundantly.

JOHN 10:10

Our Father, you are the God who pours out his love
and mercies on his people. You guide them with
your gentle, loving hand.

I want to live a full life with all the blessings, joy, and
purpose you have for me, Lord. At the end of my life, I
want to know that I have lived it well and have honored
you, served my community, and been a blessing to my
family. Help me know your abundant life. Lead me to the
scriptures that can guide me in the right direction so my
life will always stay on the course you have set for me.

Direct the steps of my family today. Help them to
see your amazing blessings in their lives and to have the
abundant life in you.

Thank you for filling our days with purpose and
blessings and joy.

In Jesus' name, amen.

121

Bear one another's burdens, and so
fulfill the law of Christ.

GALATIANS 6:2

Heavenly Father, your yoke is easy, and your burden is light. You carry your people in times of trouble and pain.

Lord, I often forget to pray for my family and friends as I should. I'm grateful I can always pray for them wherever I am. Even when I am away from home, I can still be supportive of those who need me, those you have placed in my life. Give me the heart to see others I can help, and take my focus off my problems. Help me be a prayer warrior for those who need me.

You know the concerns and burdens my family and friends are struggling with right now. Please intercede for them, and let them feel your presence.

Thank you for hearing our prayers and placing us together to share one another's burdens.

In Christ's holy name, amen.

122

Choose for yourselves this day whom you will
serve, whether the gods which your fathers served
that were on the other side of the River, or the gods
of the Amorites, in whose land you dwell. But as
for me and my house, we will serve the LORD.

JOSHUA 24:15

Almighty God, you are worthy of all worship and honor. You are the only true God, the King of the universe.

Lord, help me follow you with my whole heart. Give me the passion and courage to choose to serve you all my days. May I have the boldness to stand strong regardless of what others think. May I not be swayed by people's opinions or the way the wind is blowing in our culture and the world around us. Help me stand firm with you.

Lord, strengthen my loved ones to serve you only. Guide my family to be committed to you so that we stand together, proclaiming your Word.

Thank you for strengthening our faith and our resolve to follow you. Thank you for your faithfulness.

In Jesus' name I pray, amen.

PRAYERS *for* INSPIRATION AND ENCOURAGEMENT

123

Speak to each other with psalms, hymns, and spiritual songs, singing and making music in your hearts to the Lord. Always give thanks to God the Father for everything, in the name of our Lord Jesus Christ.

EPHESIANS 5:19–20 NCV

Heavenly Father, you are the great provider, and you always take care of me. You give me a reason to sing.

When I have good days, let me have a thankful heart. When my days are long and I'm tired, give me a thankful heart then too. Whether things are easy and I love my job or my work is harder than ever and I'm questioning everything, remind me to praise you.

Also remind my friends and family what a privilege it is to be your child. Give them thankful hearts for the beautiful sun shining and the moon that provides the cue to rest.

Thank you for your presence each and every day, Lord. Especially on the most difficult days, I'm grateful to have you near.

In your Son's precious name, amen.

124

You formed my inward parts;
You covered me in my mother's womb.
I will praise You, for I am fearfully and wonderfully made;
Marvelous are Your works,
And that my soul knows very well.

PSALM 139:13–14

Holy God, what you create is beautiful. You never make a mistake; everything you do is perfect.

Each person in my life is precious. Each one is a gift, and you created them exactly the way you wanted them to be. Help me see the beauty in your creation. Don't let me take any of them for granted.

Help the people in my community see your fingerprints on every individual. Let each challenge be seen as an opportunity for good; let each character trait be seen as a reflection of your glory.

As I think of all the people in my life by name, I thank you for creating them and for what you will do through them in the future.

In your name, amen.

125

*At that time the disciples came to Jesus, saying, "Who
then is greatest in the kingdom of heaven?" Then
Jesus called a little child to Him, set him in the midst
of them, and said, "Assuredly, I say to you, unless
you are converted and become as little children, you
will by no means enter the kingdom of heaven."*

MATTHEW 18:1-3

Father God, you have created so many gifts in this
world. Praise your precious name!

Give me wisdom to know how to love everyone in
my life, even in the tough moments. Give me patience to
deal with unexpected situations. Fill my heart with sweet
memories created with each person.

Bless each person in my life, especially those in
troubled situations. Let them feel my love and attention,
and please protect them. Show me how to point them to
you: their ever-loving, steady, dependable guide.

In Jesus' name, amen.

126

Through the LORD's mercies we are not consumed,
Because His compassions fail not.
They are new every morning;
Great is Your faithfulness.
"The LORD is my portion," says my soul,
"Therefore I hope in Him!"

LAMENTATIONS 3:22-24

You are the great I AM—eternal and unchanging—yet your mercy is always fresh and new. Magnificent is your holy name!

Whether it's the dawning of a new day, a new beginning, or a new job, give me excitement about the opportunity in each new situation. Remind me that being a follower of Christ means I have the chance every day to change a life.

Prompt me to take advantage of new opportunities as they help shape me into the person you designed me to be. Help me discern good decision making and find delight in each day.

Thank you for new mercies. Thank you for years filled with opportunities and the chance to do something great.

In your name, amen.

127

Whether you turn to the right or to the left,
your ears will hear a voice behind you,
saying, "This is the way; walk in it."

ISAIAH 30:21 NIV

Mighty God, you are omniscient. You know all, see all, and understand all things. You created everything in your time and for your purpose.

Sometimes I feel as though I have no idea what I'm doing. There are days I worry that I'm failing, that maybe I've even chosen the wrong career. Would you remind me I'm not alone? Let me hear your voice and your words of soothing reassurance.

When my friends and family are confused and feel lost, please whisper hints of your love, reassuring them that, no matter what, you are always present and are in control.

Thank you for being the Lord of my life. Thank you for guiding me each moment and for demonstrating your eternal love.

In Christ's name, amen.

128

*The LORD your God is with you, the Mighty
Warrior who saves. He will take great delight
in you; in his love he will no longer rebuke you,
but will rejoice over you with singing.*

ZEPHANIAH 3:17 NIV

Holy Father, your love is endless. You know everything about me—the pleasures and burdens of my heart—and you sing songs of joy over me.

Some days are perfect. My family and friends are happy and well, and I am reminded of my many blessings. Prompt me to thank you and to share my joy with those around me.

Bless my family and friends with many good days. Remind them of your goodness, why your Word is important, and give them reasons to have happiness in their hearts. Let them delight in you.

Thank you for the good days. Thank you for making joy contagious.

In your glorious name, amen.

129

He will yet fill your mouth with laughter
and your lips with shouts of joy.

JOB 8:21 NIV

Lord, you reign over all things and delight in your creation.

You have given me a gift in each of my friends. Their joy is infectious and their laughter contagious. Their humor is often just what I need to get through a tough day, and I praise you for that.

Help my friends find enjoyment in what they do and in your creation. Let the joy resonate in their hearts.

Thank you for laughter and its healing properties. Thank you for the memories made with my friends every day.

In the name of Jesus, amen.

130

Be strong and take heart,
all you who hope in the LORD.

PSALM 31:24 NIV

Precious Lord, you are faithful and true, and you never change.

It feels as if the world changes all the time—new ideas, new laws, new requirements. In a shifting world remind me that my hope is in you. I don't want to misplace my faith by putting it in man-made standards. I want my faith firmly grounded in your standards, your promises, and your truth.

When I am caught up in the swirl of change, along with my family and friends, remind us to be strong and faithful. When we are stressed and exhausted, help us remember our true worth as children of God.

Thank you for never changing and for always keeping your promises. I know you have the world in your hands.

In Jesus' name, amen.

131

Let the beauty of the LORD our God be upon us,
And establish the work of our hands for us;
Yes, establish the work of our hands.

PSALM 90:17

Everlasting Father, your works are wonderful, and your glory is limitless.

In everything I do—at home, at school, in the community—bless my work. Only you can see inside my heart and know that I want to do a good job and be a witness for you. Give me the ability to work and to love and to take advantage of each opportunity you send me. Remind me that others are counting on me to work hard and do well.

Help my colleagues and other staff in our organization see the importance of their jobs as they go into work every day. Give them a daily dose of joy and excitement for their tasks.

Thank you for entrusting me with the pleasure and responsibility of meaningful work.

In your Son's precious name, amen.

PRAYERS *for* INTEGRITY

132

The righteous lead blameless lives;
blessed are their children after them.

PROVERBS 20:7 NIV

Heavenly Father, you love righteousness and justice. You have set before us what is right, true, and good. I praise your holy name!

Help me live a life of integrity and honor. I feel as though I fail so often. Forgive me, and strengthen my desire to follow your Word. Restore my spirit so I will always seek to do your will. I want to be an example to my family and those around me so that, through your work in me, they will want to follow you too.

Pour your Spirit on my family and friends today. Guide them to your truth, and help them come to know you better. Reassure them that you will never leave their side.

Thank you for giving us the Scriptures so we can know more about you, your law, and your character. I am grateful you have made your will known.

In Jesus' name, amen.

133

*Let your conduct be without covetousness; be
content with such things as you have.*

HEBREWS 13:5

God, every good and perfect gift is from you. You
know exactly what your people desire and need.
You are the Great Provider.

I really struggle with wanting more than I have.
Forgive me, and show me how to be content with the
blessings you have given me so I don't complain about
what I don't have. Teach me to appreciate all you have
done for me.

My family struggles with this too. The constant
desire to have more and more can overwhelm all of us at
times. Please reveal yourself to us, and help us find our
fulfillment in you.

Thank you for always taking care of me. I am grateful for my health, my job, my family, and all the other
good things you allow in my life.

In your Son's name, amen.

134

Whatever you do, do it heartily, as to the Lord and not to men, knowing that from the Lord you will receive the reward of the inheritance; for you serve the Lord Christ.

COLOSSIANS 3:23-24

Father, you are compassionate and gracious, slow to anger, and abounding in love. You have removed our sins as far as the east is from the west. How great is your unfailing love!

Some days are difficult, and I can become discouraged about my job. When that happens, help me regain my priorities and focus. Remind me why I serve you and whom I am really doing this for. Change my attitude toward the work you have called me to do. Help me be passionate and professional in my responsibilities because I ultimately do the work for you.

Please continue to be with my family. Bless them as they, too, work for you. Increase their joy today.

Thank you for allowing me to follow my passion and you. Thank you for showing me how important it is to work with honor and distinction.

In your holy name, amen.

135

Above all else, guard your heart,
for everything you do flows from it.

PROVERBS 4:23 NIV

Lord, you have established your throne in heaven, and your kingdom is all the earth. I worship your holy name.

Forgive me for looking at images with lust and filling my mind and heart with things I shouldn't. Give me strength to resist the lure of sin that can be ever present on the computer, television, and so many other places. Guard my heart, and repair my spirit so I may live a godly life in all areas.

Protect the hearts of my family too. Keep the children pure, and don't let the Evil One get a foothold in their lives. Give them wisdom and sound judgment so they will live honorably.

Thank you for being a forgiving God. I am so grateful to know that when I stumble and fall, you will pick me up and clean me off. Thank you for never giving up on me.

In Christ's name, amen.

136

Honor all people. Love the brotherhood.
Fear God. Honor the king.

1 PETER 2:17

Gracious Father, you are the King of kings and Lord of lords. Your majesty covers all the earth. I will serve you all my days.

Lord, please give me the humility and grace to serve those in authority over me. Remove any pride or conceit that would get in the way of doing my job and keeping my promises. Use my life to continually guide others to you.

Help the people in my business unit stay positive and respectful toward authority. Sometimes we criticize and disrespect our leaders behind their backs. Guide our conversations and attitudes so that we give the respect due to those in charge. Let humility grow in our hearts.

Thank you for your continued guidance.

In Jesus' name, amen.

137

Do not be conformed to this world, but be
transformed by the renewing of your mind.

ROMANS 12:2

Father, you sit on your high throne surrounded by the angels, and yet you still teach us what is good and pleasing to you. Your gentle love can never be matched.

I feel bombarded by the world sometimes. Keep your Word and teachings fresh in my mind so I will not be deceived by the Evil One. Help me stay focused on reading the Bible, and let it sink into my soul. I need to have your desires in the forefront of my mind.

Teach your Word and desires to my friends and family. Let studying Scripture be a priority for them, and give them the wisdom and understanding to make it real in their lives.

Thank you for showing us what is good and true. I am so grateful you have given us instructions on what is best for us.

In Jesus' name, amen.

138

*No temptation has overtaken you except such as
is common to man; but God is faithful, who will
not allow you to be tempted beyond what you are
able, but with the temptation will also make the
way of escape, that you may be able to bear it.*

1 CORINTHIANS 10:13

Heavenly Father, you are faithful and just. You keep your promises of love for a thousand generations.

Temptation waits for me around every corner. Because of the television, the computer, and my own sinful heart, I struggle with desires to look at things or to act in ways I know are contrary to your will. Please forgive me and strengthen me to face those battles. When temptations come, help me have the wisdom and strength to avoid them. Place your Word in my heart so I will strive to live for you.

Protect my friends and family today. So many things vie for their attention. Keep the schemes of the Evil One from them, and let their desires always be to please you.

Thank you for your promise to help us with our temptations and struggles.

In Jesus' name, amen.

139

*In all things showing yourself to be a pattern of good
works; in doctrine showing integrity, reverence,
incorruptibility, sound speech that cannot be
condemned, that one who is an opponent may be
ashamed, having nothing evil to say of you.*

TITUS 2:7–8

Father, you do not treat your people as they deserve,
but you are gracious and merciful, patient and forgiving. I am humbled by your amazing pardon of all
our sins.

Let your integrity and character flow through me. So
many people I know and work with don't know you. Help
me keep my behavior consistent with being a Christian
so they might see you through me. Provide opportunities
to share your love with those around me.

Instill in my family your thoughts and wishes. May
we always keep them at the forefront of our home. Guide
us to seek your plan for our lives, and be with us today as
we go our separate ways.

Thank you for showing us what is right in your sight.
In Jesus' name, amen.

140

Flee also youthful lusts; but pursue
righteousness, faith, love, peace with those
who call on the Lord out of a pure heart.

2 TIMOTHY 2:22

God, you assemble your people from all around the world. You are the Good Shepherd, who gathers and protects his flock.

Help me win the battle against lust. I struggle with habits and thoughts I know you don't want me to engage in. At times I feel powerless. Guide me to a strong Christian friend to whom I can be accountable. Help me have victory over this battle.

Protect my home and my family from destructive forces. Keep us safe and guard our hearts. Give us wisdom on how to make our home a pure and secure place.

I am thankful you have given us a community of believers who help and encourage one another. Thank you that, because of that community and your faithful presence, I am not alone in this.

In Jesus' name, amen.

141

Blessed is the man who fears the LORD,
Who delights greatly in His commandments.
His descendants will be mighty on earth;
The generation of the upright will be blessed.

PSALM 112:1-2

Almighty Lord, the depth of your wisdom knows no end. The magnitude of your plans is immeasurable. Great and mighty are you!

Help me be fully committed to your words and commandments. Fill me with the Holy Spirit and the desire to do your will at all times. Guide me to be a godly person of integrity so I will live for you and know your blessings.

I earnestly want my friends and family to have a strong relationship with you, to follow you out of love and reverence all their days. Have mercy on them, and give them your grace to know you.

Thank you for giving us the power to follow you even when we don't think we can. I am grateful for the Holy Spirit, who gently guides me.

In your Son's name, amen.

142

If it is possible, as much as depends on
you, live peaceably with all men.

ROMANS 12:18

Almighty God, we will celebrate the abundance of your goodness and will shout for joy because of your overflowing grace.

Keep me from the petty conflicts that can interrupt my life and don't reflect well on you. Help me be a peacemaker. Show me the people I need to go to and heal a division. Empower me to walk in integrity for your name's sake.

Bless our marriage by removing any conflicts between my spouse and me, and keep the Evil One from stirring up tension and strife. Teach us both to rely on you and your instruction. Place your calming spirit in our home.

I am grateful you show us the way that is good and true. Thank you for being the Prince of Peace.

In Christ's name, amen.

143

Create in me a clean heart, O God,
And renew a steadfast spirit within me.

PSALM 51:10

Our Father in heaven, you are the great Redeemer. You reached down from heaven and saved humanity by your own mighty hand. Your love can never be matched.

I feel overwhelmed and ashamed by my sin. As much as I struggle and fight, I still stumble and fall far too often. Please forgive me. You know my heart better than I do. Cleanse me and renew me so I have a fresh spirit within me.

Remind my family today that you are the God who restores souls and heals wounds. Teach them never to be afraid to approach you and ask for forgiveness.

Thank you for taking pleasure in reconciling your people. I am so grateful to serve a God who continues to love us regardless of how many times we mess up.

In your Son's name, amen.

PRAYERS *for* LOVE AND MARRIAGE

144

I have learned in whatever state I am, to be content.

PHILIPPIANS 4:11

Lord, your law is perfect and converts the soul. Your testimony is pure and wise. You are the defender of all who trust in you.

I am bombarded with messages every day that say I need more things to make me happy and satisfied. Help me not to listen to those messages or to be preoccupied by what others have. Teach me to find my fulfillment in you, not in bigger houses and more toys. Show me what true contentment is.

Please help my spouse and me to be united in how we manage our money and resources. Remind us to be open and honest with each other in this area. Keep our desires in check so we're not chasing after the next best thing. Instead, fill our family with thanksgiving and satisfaction.

Thank you for providing all we truly need and teaching us what we don't need. Thank you for being the source of balance in a hectic world.

In Jesus' holy name, amen.

145

There is no fear in love; but perfect love casts out fear.

1 JOHN 4:18

Heavenly Father, only your love is perfect. It never fails. It is always right. It casts out fear.

I need your love for my spouse. When I get busy or stressed, I don't always show the depth of my love. Let your love flow through me to my life partner.

Love my spouse today in a way that is tangible. Cast out any fear with your perfect love.

Thank you that your love is unfailing even when mine fails. I'm so grateful for my spouse you have given me. Help me demonstrate that today.

In your name I pray, amen.

146

"The mountains shall depart
And the hills be removed,
But My kindness shall not depart from you,
Nor shall My covenant of peace be removed,"
Says the LORD, who has mercy on you.

ISAIAH 54:10

Dear Father, you stay true to your promises. You do not break your word, and your love is steadfast.

Show us how to be more loving and caring. Show us how to encourage, how to support, and how to enjoy the gift of marriage. Father, please guard my spouse's heart, and mine as well. Bring us closer to you and to each other. Give us a supernatural love for each other.

Thank you that you are the ultimate covenant maker and keeper.

In Jesus' holy name, amen.

147

Now to Him who is able to do exceedingly abundantly above all that we ask or think, according to the power that works in us, to Him be glory in the church by Christ Jesus to all generations, forever and ever. Amen.

EPHESIANS 3:20–21

Father, you are able to do more than I could ever ask or imagine.

There are parts of my marriage that feel broken beyond repair. I ask for your restoration and your love to do more than I ever thought possible in our relationship.

Protect those around us who are affected by our struggles, especially our close family. Surround them and give us discernment when we are speaking to them.

Thank you that you still perform miracles and that your love brings restoration to all generations. Our family members are part of that promise, and I'm so thankful to see that playing out in their lives even now.

In Jesus' name, amen.

148

I say to you, if you have faith as a mustard seed, you
will say to this mountain, "Move from here to there," and
it will move; and nothing will be impossible for you.

MATTHEW 17:20

Dear God, you created the world from the highest of the heavens to the depths of the sea. You know each detail of your creation.

Grow my faith today, for it is weak. Marital problems and disagreements in our home make me weary. Move mountains in my heart. Move mountains in my family.

God, be with my spouse today. Fill us both with peace and understanding for each other and for our family.

Thank you for still moving mountains and accepting my faith no matter the state of it. I'm grateful for my spouse's understanding and support. I feel treasured and cherished when my partner protects me and shows me just how much I am loved.

In Jesus' name, amen.

149

The LORD will fight for you, and
you shall hold your peace.

EXODUS 14:14

God above, you fight for us. You are the ultimate victor in every battle.

Remind me today, Father, that this battle isn't my own. When I get defensive with my spouse or want to prove myself the winner of each argument, remind me that this is not my battle; it's yours.

Fight for my family today. When the Enemy tries to steal our joy, fight for us. When the Enemy tries to tell us we aren't good enough, fight for us.

Thank you for fighting on behalf of my family.

In your name I pray, amen.

150

Beloved, do not avenge yourselves, but rather
give place to wrath; for it is written, "Vengeance
is Mine, I will repay," says the Lord.

ROMANS 12:19

God, your judgments are made in perfect love. I can't argue with your perfect will.

Set my eyes and my heart on you today. I am holding on to grudges against my spouse, and I want to let them go. Teach me to leave my hurts with you.

Fill my spouse with unexpected grace today for me and for our family. May my spouse's heart be soft toward you, and may your love refresh my partner's spirit.

I give you thanks for your faithfulness. It is sure and strong and never ending.

In Jesus' name, amen.

151

Now all things are of God, who has reconciled
us to Himself through Jesus Christ, and has
given us the ministry of reconciliation.

2 CORINTHIANS 5:18

Father of light, you are in the business of reconciliation. You bring peace and hope even in the most desperate circumstances.

Give me the desire to reconcile with my spouse when we argue. It is easier to remain angry and refuse to forgive. Bring us peace, and let your love overflow in my life.

Fill my spouse and me with patience and grace. When we are at odds with each other, remind us that you can heal all wounds.

Thank you for the gift of grace and its power to transform relationships. Thank you for the work you've done already in my marriage and the joy you've given us. When my spouse surprises me with an especially kind gesture, I marvel at your goodness in putting that wonderful human in my life.

It's in Christ's name I pray, amen.

152

He will give the rain for your seed
With which you sow the ground,
And bread of the increase of the earth;
It will be fat and plentiful.

ISAIAH 30:23

Loving Father, your harvest is bountiful. You give me the delight of seeing my spouse grow and change daily. Only you deserve glory and honor and praise.

Rain down your mercy upon me, so my legacy will be a quality life sprinkled with kindness, compassion, and a sense of humor. Let our home be remembered as a joyous, safe place.

Please help my partner feel your loving presence in all areas of life. When my spouse feels out of place or alone, remind my spouse that you are ever-present.

Thank you for loving us enough to nurture us through your Word.

In your name, amen.

153

But the fruit of the Spirit is love, joy, peace,
longsuffering, kindness, goodness, faithfulness,
gentleness, self-control. Against such there is no law.

GALATIANS 5:22–23

Heavenly Father, you are the source of joy, peace, and love, which is shown through your Son's sacrifice on the cross.

On the days when my patience is thin, when I fear I'll express my frustration, remind me of your mercy toward me. Take away the frazzled feelings of stress, and replace them with heaping portions of self-control seasoned with patience and flavored with kindness.

When my partner has no more patience, please provide yours. Remind my spouse that you see each stressful situation and each moment of frustration.

Thank you for setting an example for us through your Son, who lived out the fruit of the Spirit in every way. Thank you for making me more like him every day.

In his precious name, amen.

154

Bear with each other and forgive one another if any of you has a grievance against someone. Forgive as the Lord forgave you. And over all these virtues put on love, which binds them all together in perfect unity.

COLOSSIANS 3:13–14 NIV

F ather, your forgiveness stretches as far as the east is from the west. You humble me with your love.

When I'm hurt, it's sometimes difficult for me to let it go. If my spouse is critical of me, I want to hold a grudge. Soften my heart with whispered reminders of your grace and forgiveness. Remind me that the point is not whether someone else deserves mercy—because I'm a sinner in need of mercy too.

God, help us love each other. Help us get along and form a God-honoring relationship. Bless the love I have for my spouse and guide us to work through problems with compassion and understanding.

Thank you for making the ultimate sacrifice for unworthy human hearts. Thank you for loving your creation that much.

In Jesus' name, amen.

155

Beloved, if God so loved us, we also ought to love one another. No one has seen God at any time. If we love one another, God abides in us, and His love has been perfected in us.

1 JOHN 4:11-12

God, your love covers all sin, and it washes us white as snow.

Help me love my spouse who can sometimes seem unlovable. Some days I want to pretend my partner's not there. Soften my heart so I can see my spouse through your eyes. Give me wisdom and compassion.

Father, touch my spouse's heart. Teach my partner through my actions that you are a mighty God, who loves unconditionally. Let me be your example.

Thank you for loving me when I'm unlovable. Thank you for forgiving me and for seeing my soul and finding it worthy of salvation.

In your Son's name, amen.

156

*The things which you learned and received
and heard and saw in me, these do, and
the God of peace will be with you.*

PHILIPPIANS 4:9

God, all glory and honor be to you, who gave us Jesus, our Savior!

As I learn from your Word, let me put that wisdom into practice in my marriage. Help me improve my marriage by having high expectations for myself. I want to handle my marriage wisely, as you handle me.

I pray that my spouse will grow closer to you and apply your Word to our marriage.

Thank you for loving me enough to guide my footsteps. Thank you for reminding me that applying your truths helps me grow in your love.

In your holy name, amen.

157

Though one may be overpowered by
another, two can withstand him.
And a threefold cord is not quickly broken.
ECCLESIASTES 4:12

F ather in heaven, you are the fountain of truth, and you make constant declarations of your love.

Remind me that when I have a good idea or a successful strategy, I can support my spouse by sharing it. Help me do that in a spirit of love, offering aid and collaboration without appearing as if I think I have it all figured out.

Let my spouse be open to sharing with me. Humble us, open our hearts, and keep us grounded in the spirit of being a family.

Thank you for your love. Thank you for teaching us how to give and receive and for making us better through collaboration.

In your name, amen.

158

A new commandment I give to you, that you love
one another; as I have loved you, that you also
love one another. By this all will know that you are
My disciples, if you have love for one another.

JOHN 13:34–35

Dear God, you are love. I know this because your Word says so, and I know this because I know that you love me so much.

Help me love other people the way you love them. When a new relationship starts for me, don't let me get caught up in what the world says is love. Teach me what real love is.

Show your love to the people in my life. Fill them up with it until your love is all they need.

Thank you for loving us no matter where we come from, who we are, or what we do.

In Jesus' name, amen.

159

Walk worthy of the calling with which you were called,
with all lowliness and gentleness, with longsuffering,
bearing with one another in love, endeavoring to
keep the unity of the Spirit in the bond of peace.

EPHESIANS 4:1-3

Father, you sent your Son to serve us here on earth even though we didn't deserve it. But you loved us so much you did it anyway.

Forgive me for my selfishness, especially in my relationships with friends and loved ones. I think about me most of the time, but help me think about you and others first.

I know so many wonderful servant-hearted people. Please give them the encouragement and energy they need to keep serving and loving people.

Thank you for these good examples you have put in my life.

In Christ I pray, amen.

PRAYERS *for* MY FUTURE

160

*God began doing a good work in you, and
I am sure he will continue it until it is
finished when Jesus Christ comes again.*

PHILIPPIANS 1:6 NCV

Father, you direct my path. You know everything about my future, and you care about me.

Today I feel overwhelmed by decisions I need to make. I'm not sure which way to go, and it feels like too much to handle. Show me the best choice in every situation.

Be with my family today. Show them that they can trust you no matter how hard or confusing life is right now.

Thank you for being a good Father I can trust each day. Thank you for listening to me.

In Jesus' name, amen.

161

Therefore I say to you, whatever things you ask when you pray, believe that you receive them, and you will have them.

MARK 11:24

Dear God, you are wise, loving, and generous. You don't hold back any good thing from me or any of your children.

I ask for wisdom in this season of life. Guide me as I walk through my day, meet new people, and have new experiences. Make me wiser as I get to know you better.

When situations arise, remind me to ask you about decisions, before anyone else, so I will make wise choices and deepen my relationship with you.

I'm grateful for these new opportunities to grow and to learn.

In Christ I pray, amen.

162

For I know the thoughts that I think toward you, says the LORD, thoughts of peace and not of evil, to give you a future and a hope.

JEREMIAH 29:11

Dear Father, you are the God of hope. You are the God of my past, present, and future.

Sometimes things are confusing and hard. Right now it's hard for me to believe I have a bright future. Help me have hope, and show me the good things you have planned for me.

Comfort my friends and those in my family who feel lost. Bring them peace when they feel restless; bring them hope when they feel discouraged and alone.

Thank you for your plan for me even though I don't yet know what it is.

In Jesus' name, amen.

163

*Now this is the confidence that we have in Him, that if
we ask anything according to His will, He hears us. And
if we know that He hears us, whatever we ask, we know
that we have the petitions that we have asked of Him.*

1 JOHN 5:14–15

God, you hear all my prayers. You are kind, understanding, and faithful. You never get tired of
listening to me.

Father, help me understand what next step I should
take for my future. Show me when I read my Bible. Show
me when I talk to wise friends and mentors. You have
promised to answer when we come to you in prayer.

I know people who are angry because they didn't
receive the answer they'd hoped for. Help them feel your
love for them; remind them that you always hear their
prayers—even when your plans are different from theirs.

Thank you for reminding me that there is a purpose
in each answered and unanswered prayer.

It's in Jesus' name I pray, amen.

164

You shall walk after the LORD your God and fear
Him, and keep His commandments and obey His
voice; you shall serve Him and hold fast to Him.

DEUTERONOMY 13:4

Good Father, I hear so many voices in my head telling me what to do next with my life that I don't know which one to trust. Help me know which voice is yours, the only trustworthy voice.

Give me courage to do what you are asking, to trust that you know what is best. I pray this season will increase my faith so that I may hear your voice more clearly.

Thank you for being with me during this time of change and for promising that you will be with me forever.

In Jesus' name, amen.

165

But the wisdom that is from above is first
pure, then peaceable, gentle, willing to
yield, full of mercy and good fruits.
JAMES 3:17

Dear God, every gift from you is perfect. There is nothing bad in you. You never make mistakes.

Let this be a year of renewal, of following you more intentionally, more joyfully. May my life show the fruit of the Spirit to those around me so they will truly see you in me.

Teach me what I need to know to shine the light of grace to others, to witness to people around me, to speak kindness and encouragement to those I meet along the way. Help me grow in your love in the days ahead.

In Christ I pray, amen.

166

Let your light so shine before men, that they may see
your good works and glorify your Father in heaven.

MATTHEW 5:16

Father, you are everywhere all the time. Even in my darkest moments you shine through, and I can see you.

God, help me be a light today everywhere I go. I feel as if sometimes I'm the only one in my circle who knows you, and it can be hard to keep following you. Help me stand up for you, no matter what, so you will be glorified.

I want the people I encounter to know you. Work on their hearts. Give them a desire to learn about you and the Bible. Show them how much you love them.

Thank you for the people I've met and for those I've yet to meet.

In your name I pray, amen.

167

Seek first the kingdom of God and His righteousness,
and all these things shall be added to you.

MATTHEW 6:33

D ear God, you are the reason for everything I do. Without you, I have no purpose.

Sometimes I get caught up in work and in wanting to please my boss and the people around me. Change my heart, God. Help me want to please you first, because you matter above all else

I pray for my boss and the other supervisors at work. Take away the pressure they feel, and help them lean on you.

Thank you for being with me even when I'm not focused on you.

In Jesus' name, amen.

168

*I have shown you in every way, by laboring
like this, that you must support the weak. And
remember the words of the Lord Jesus, that He
said, "It is more blessed to give than to receive."*

ACTS 20:35

Dear God, you gave us the best gift of all: your Son.
You sacrificed everything to be near us.

Forgive me for allowing worry about my job to
replace service to others. Forgive me for forgetting to
care for the people you've place in my life coworkers,
family, friends, and people in my community whose
needs are great. Give me a servant heart.

Be close to those who don't have a home or a family
or work to do. Remind them that they are your children
and are important in your eyes.

Thank you for loving all your children.

In Jesus' name, amen.

169

Listen to counsel and receive instruction,
That you may be wise in your latter days.
There are many plans in a man's heart,
Nevertheless the LORD's counsel—that will stand.

PROVERBS 19:20-21

F ather, your Word will last forever. Everything you say is true and full of love.

I need forgiveness for being willful, for following my own plans. Focusing on my selfish desires leads to disappointment. Help me see your will and walk in it. Please increase my desire to follow your plan for my life. Help me know what that plan is.

Sometimes I feel helpless because of the uncertainties in life, and I contemplate what to do next. Please continue to give me unexpected opportunities and everlasting hope.

Thank you for your forgiveness and your faithfulness. In Christ's name, amen.

170

Remind them to be subject to rulers and
authorities, to obey, to be ready for every good
work, to speak evil of no one, to be peaceable,
gentle, showing all humility to all men.

TITUS 3:1-2

Dear Father, you are a good ruler. You are fair, and you want justice. I can trust in your good judgment.

Humble me today. I am struggling with authority in my life and at work. It's hard for me to follow a leader I don't respect or trust. Give me wisdom, and help me let go of this situation and give it to you to handle.

I pray for the people you have placed in authority over me. Show them how to lead with kindness and courage.

Thank you for caring about every detail of my life both today and in the future.

In Jesus' name, amen.

171

Repay no one evil for evil. Have regard for good things in the sight of all men. If it is possible, as much as depends on you, live peaceably with all men. Beloved, do not avenge yourselves, but rather give place to wrath; for it is written, "Vengeance is Mine, I will repay," says the Lord.

ROMANS 12:17–19

Dear God, you are sovereign. Nothing happens that you don't know about or care about. You see it all.

I need your peace right now. I feel that I've been wronged and blamed for things I haven't done, and I'm afraid I'll lose the respect of friends and coworkers. I surrender these feelings to you. I know that you're the final judge and that you want good things for my life.

Be with my family during this time. Give them hope and faith in you and in me. Make them stronger, and give them joy in the middle of the stressful times.

Thank you for your mercies and your promises.

In Jesus' name, amen.

172

My beloved brethren, be steadfast, immovable,
always abounding in the work of the Lord, knowing
that your labor is not in vain in the Lord.

1 CORINTHIANS 15:58

God, you can redeem anything. You can turn around even the worst situation and make it better than I could imagine.

Give me hope in my job. It's not exactly what I thought it would be, and I don't always feel motivated and excited by it. Remind me that anything I do is for you, so I should do it with all my heart. Remind me often that this is the first step on a new life path.

I have friends who don't love their jobs right now. Remind them to work joyfully because you love them, not because they have their dream jobs.

I am so grateful your plan is better than mine.

In Christ I pray, amen.

173

Don't be carried away by all kind of strange teachings.
It is good for our hearts to be strengthened by grace.

HEBREWS 13:9 NIV

God, you really are all that I need. Your grace is sufficient for me.

I often feel as though I don't know what I'm doing. I'm afraid of failing. But, Lord, I know that your strength is made perfect in my weakness, so please be my strength today.

Some of my family members need to be reminded of your grace. They work so hard, but it never feels like enough. Show them your grace—a gift they don't have to earn.

Thank you for your grace and your strength, which lift me up and give me hope for the future.

In your name, amen.

PRAYERS *for* PARENTHOOD

174

No discipline seems pleasant at the time, but painful.
Later on, however, it produces a harvest of righteousness
and peace for those who have been trained by it.

HEBREWS 12:11 NIV

Dear Father, you are righteous and worthy of my praise. You are the one true God, and I am in awe of you.

Sometimes I struggle with how to parent my children. They need discipline, and they need love, and I don't always know how to balance those things. Show me the way in this.

Be with my children when they fight and disagree. Give them a godly love for one another and deeper understanding and appreciation for our family.

Thank you for the unexpected delights of parenthood. Thank you for morning snuggles and evening laughter and for being with us throughout the day.

In Jesus' name, amen.

175

Behold, children are a heritage from the LORD,
The fruit of the womb is a reward.

PSALM 127:3

Almighty God, your love is immeasurable. Your love is so great that you sent your one and only Son to die for me and my family.

I have so many worries about my children and whether or not I'm a good parent to them. I love them so much and want the very best for them, but I often doubt myself and my parenting skills. Grant me your peace as I strive to do my best, and give me the wisdom, discernment, and confidence to make the right decisions for them.

Be with us today as we guide and love our children. Give us the patience and insight we need to guide our family through this day.

Thank you for the blessing and joy of being a parent. Most of all, thank you for loving my children more than I ever could.

In Christ's name I pray, amen.

176

Rejoice in the Lord always.
Again I will say, rejoice!

PHILIPPIANS 4:4

Lord, you are the God of heaven and earth. You see from the beginning to the end and have made us to be with you for eternity. May we forever praise your name!

I want to remain focused on you and the pleasure of knowing that I will be with you always. Don't let the Evil One cloud my thoughts and steal the sheer joy of being one of your children. Keep my eyes and thoughts on the eternity I will spend with you.

Walk with me today and always. Teach me to appreciate and enjoy your many blessings, including my children. Remind them that you will always be there for them, even if I am not.

Thank you for saving and loving me. Thank you for pouring your Spirit into me and giving me a tiny glimpse now of what it will be like with you in heaven.

In Christ's name, amen.

177

A soft answer turns away wrath,
But a harsh word stirs up anger.

PROVERBS 15:1

Heavenly Father, you speak to us in gentle whispers, and yet your words carry the power of eternal life. I am in awe of your mighty ways.

Sometimes I say things to my children I later regret. Remind me of the impact my words have on them. Forgive me and heal any wounds I have caused. Guide my thoughts and words so I will encourage my children and not tear them down. Soften my heart and how I express myself.

Lift my children's spirits today. Bless them with your encouragement, and build them up by giving them a joy and a reverence for you. Let kindness and gentleness flow through our home.

Thank you for taming my tongue and giving me a desire to gently cultivate my children's spirits. I am so grateful you have given these children to me.

In your Son's name, amen.

178

He will turn the hearts of the parents to their children,
and the hearts of the children to their parents.

MALACHI 4:6 NIV

Father, you are a loving and forgiving God. You are our advocate and our redeemer. You deal righteously and compassionately with your people.

Teach me to forgive as you do and to model that kind of grace and mercy for my spouse and children. Help me be the kind of parent my family can always turn to without fearing my reaction. Strengthen our love for one another and you.

Work in my children's hearts to have the spirit of repentance. Help us be open and honest in our relationships, and guide us to follow your example when we are wronged or hurt.

I am grateful for your grace and mercy in our lives. Thank you for drawing us to you and making true forgiveness possible.

In Jesus' name, amen.

179

Now may the God of hope fill you with all joy
and peace in believing, that you may abound
in hope by the power of the Holy Spirit.

ROMANS 15:13

Heavenly Father, you turn our sorrows into dancing and our defeats into celebrations. You are the God who refreshes his people.

Even though I have many reasons to be jubilant and appreciative, I focus too often on the negative and dark things in my life. Fill me again with your joy and peace and an appreciation for your blessings. Teach me how to have fun and take pleasure in the life you have given me.

My family needs your constant presence. When my children are older, let them remember that our home was filled with happiness and laughter. Give them eyes to search for joy regardless of their circumstances.

Thank you for the gift of joy and happiness and all the pleasures associated with being your child.

In Jesus' name, amen.

180

These words which I command you today shall
be in your heart. You shall teach them diligently
to your children, and shall talk of them when
you sit in your house, when you walk by the way,
when you lie down, and when you rise up.

DEUTERONOMY 6:6–7

God, you are the maker of heaven and earth, the all-powerful Creator. You are worthy of all praise and honor.

Fill me with your Spirit and your mind. Help me communicate your words and commands to my children. Guide my thoughts and our conversations so that, as a family, we will talk more about you and learn more about you. Teach me to be a godly example for my children so they will be encouraged to follow you.

Reach down and touch my children's hearts, Lord. Open their ears and their hearts to your words and your heart, and remove any barriers that the Evil One puts in their way.

Thank you for my children's love and for allowing me to raise them. I am grateful for the opportunity to tell them about you.

In Jesus' name, amen.

PRAYERS *for* PATIENCE AND BALANCE

181

Wait on the LORD;
Be of good courage,
And He shall strengthen your heart;
Wait, I say, on the LORD!

PSALM 27:14

Heavenly Father, you are slow to anger and compassionate and long suffering. Your timing is perfect, and your ways are right.

Forgive me for being impatient and forgetting that you are guiding my steps. Give me peace to be content with your timing and direct every corner of my life. Subdue my desire to control everything; teach me to wait for and listen to your voice.

Bring a calm spirit to our home today, and let my family and friends rest in your gentle care. May we take small, steady steps toward a mature faith.

Thank you for doing what is best for us in your timing, not ours, as you watch over our lives.

In Jesus' name, amen.

182

For whatever things were written before were written
for our learning, that we through the patience and
comfort of the Scriptures might have hope.

ROMANS 15:4

Lord, you spoke the foundations of the earth and all the heavens into existence. You are eternal and unchanging. You are the magnificent Creator!

There are days when hope feels very far away, when it seems as if nothing matters and everything is out of control. Help me fight these feelings and rely instead on what you have promised—that you have a plan for me and it is good.

Remind my family and friends today that you have a plan for all of us. Comfort them with the knowledge that you are in control and everything you do is for our good. Soothe our spirits, and let us be united as we seek your will for our lives.

Thank you for restoring our hope. I am grateful that you care enough for us to hold our futures in your hands.

In your Son's name, amen.

183

The LORD GOD is my strength.
He makes me like a deer that does not stumble
so I can walk on the steep mountains.

HABAKKUK 3:19 NCV

My Father in heaven, you are immeasurably capable of doing whatever we ask or imagine. You are worthy of all glory and honor.

I need you. Most days I feel drained of strength and desire. I try to do my best to serve my family and community, but I get worn down. Please renew my strength. Restore the energy and passion I had when I first followed you; give me the desire to live the life you have designed for me.

The hectic pace of life seems to overrun our family at times. There's always somewhere to be or something to do. Even church functions and serving others can be exhausting. Father, will you refresh us so we can better serve you and others?

You are our source of strength in chaotic times. Thank you for being our ever-present help.

In Christ's name, amen.

184

Look carefully then how you walk, not as unwise
but as wise, making the best use of the time.

EPHESIANS 5:15–16 ESV

Father, many are the wonders you have done, and magnificent are your plans. You are great and do marvelous things!

I feel torn at times, and it seems my life gets off track. Teach me to keep my relationship with you and my responsibilities to my family as my first and foremost priorities. Help me to keep order in my life and to manage my time and treasures appropriately.

Transform my family and how we look at our schedules. We get so busy and often spend our time and attention on things that won't last. Bring stability and balance to our home.

Thank you for every season of life. I am so grateful that you want us to enjoy all the blessings you have given us.

In Jesus' holy name, amen.

185

He said to them, "Come aside by yourselves
to a deserted place and rest a while."

MARK 6:31

Dear Lord, your rest is a blessing to all who call on your name. You are the shelter and the comfort during the storms. You are the great I AM.

I am exhausted. I run myself ragged with working, taking care of my family, and trying to fulfill my obligations. Show me how to take a Sabbath and rest my body, mind, and soul so I might serve you better and be the Christian I want to be.

Remind my family what it means to slow down and take a break. Show them it is okay to take time away and rejuvenate, and help them use that time to focus on you and the life you have for them.

Thank you for not only giving us permission to rest but also showing us how.

In your name, amen.

186

Where your treasure is,
there your heart will be also.

MATTHEW 6:21

F ather, your Son is the greatest treasure from heaven. He is the ultimate gift and the mighty Savior. His name will be praised forever.

In my heart I put things above you and your will. Please forgive me. Restore my desire to place you, your wisdom, and your guidance for my life above all else. Let my treasures not be the things of this world but the good gifts you have for me.

Please help me avoid the trappings of this world. Help me keep my priorities straight and make the right decisions.

Thank you for clearing the clutter from my life and turning my attention back to you. Thank you for all your wonderful blessings.

In your Son's name, amen.

187

Whatever things are true, whatever things are noble,
whatever things are just, whatever things are pure,
whatever things are lovely, whatever things are
of good report, if there is any virtue and if there is
anything praiseworthy—meditate on these things.

PHILIPPIANS 4:8

Heavenly Father, you are the source of all that is beautiful and good. You are the wellspring of life and all that exists. Your name is worthy of all praise and honor.

I get too caught up in the negative and depressing aspects of this world, and my mind strays from you. Help me focus on the positive and good things you provide. When I drift into the negative, remind me to refocus on your character traits, and let others see in me your positive qualities.

Keep the Evil One from distorting my view of your world. Regardless of the circumstances, may I always see the beauty of your hand in my life.

Thank you for pouring out the magnificence of your character on our world. I am grateful you have given us eyes to see your work.

In Christ's name, amen.

PRAYERS *for* PEACE AND PROTECTION

188

He shall give His angels charge over you,
To keep you in all your ways.
In their hands they shall bear you up,
Lest you dash your foot against a stone.

PSALM 91:11-12

Father, you are the defender of your people and the upholder of righteousness. I am powerless without you.

I am called to dangerous places where I need your supernatural protection and guidance. Please put angels around me to guard me from the seen and unseen dangers in my life. Let them shield and guide me.

Surround my family and friends with your angelic warriors. Keep the Evil One far from them, and give my loved ones comfort in knowing that you fight for them. Protect every step they take today.

Thank you for using your army of angels to care for us and fight for us. I am grateful for the many ways you watch over my family, friends, and me.

In Christ's holy name, amen.

189

The end of a thing is better than its beginning . . .
Do not say,
"Why were the former days better than these?"
For you do not inquire wisely concerning this.
Wisdom is good with an inheritance,
And profitable to those who see the sun.

ECCLESIASTES 7:8, 10–11

Father, you are the beginning and the end. You live outside of time, and you know ahead of time everything that will happen.

I feel sad today and need your comfort. I am going through a challenging time that requires change. Restore my hope in this time of change.

Some of my friends and family don't understand why I am struggling. Help them know you have a special plan and purpose for everyone. I know that you will protect me.

Thank you for new beginnings.

In Jesus' name, amen.

190

So do not throw away your confidence;
it will be richly rewarded.
You need to persevere so that when you have done the
will of God, you will receive what he has promised.

HEBREWS 10:35–36 NIV

Dear God, your timing is perfect. You don't let anything happen too late or too early.

But I don't feel ready for this next step in life. I don't know what's ahead and that uncertainty shakes my confidence. Please, Father, replace that uncertainty with a sense of calm confidence, knowing you are leading my life. Be my rock. Remind me to lean on you.

Thank you that everything in my life can be used for your purposes.

In Christ I pray, amen.

191

One thing I do: Forgetting what is behind and
straining toward what is ahead, I press on
toward the goal to win the prize for which God
has called me heavenward in Christ Jesus.

PHILIPPIANS 3:13–14 NIV

Dear Father, you forgive and forget all my sins. You are the reason I can live without regret.

Lord, I have so many what-if questions right now. Moving forward is hard when I have questions about my past, when guilt and regret surface. Give me the courage to press on toward the goal and not look back.

Thank you for Christ, who has set us free.

In his name I pray, amen.

192

Do not remember the former things,
Nor consider the things of old.
Behold, I will do a new thing,
Now it shall spring forth;
Shall you not know it?
I will even make a road in the wilderness
And rivers in the desert.

ISAIAH 43:18-19

Father, you are the God of possibility. You make the impossible possible. You can create a river in the middle of a desert and make good things happen when I least expect them.

It's hard for me to imagine life being better than it is now. You have brought so many blessings into my life. Stay close to me as I take the next step.

Thank you for giving me rivers in the middle of my deserts. I ask you to do so again.

Thank you for the hope we have in you.

In Jesus' name, amen.

193

The Lord is my shepherd;
I shall not want.
He makes me to lie down in green pastures;
He leads me beside the still waters.
He restores my soul;
He leads me in the paths of righteousness
For His name's sake.

PSALM 23:1–3

Father, you are a good shepherd to your people. You know each one of us, and when we get lost, you come and find us.

Remind me of this again and again today: "He leads me in the paths of righteousness." When I'm not sure where my life is going or what changes are ahead, show me the right path and bring me peace.

You are the constant restorer of my soul.

Thank you for leading me with love.

In Christ's name I pray, amen.

194

Be anxious for nothing, but in everything by prayer
and supplication, with thanksgiving, let your
requests be made known to God; and the peace of
God, which surpasses all understanding, will guard
your hearts and minds through Christ Jesus.

PHILIPPIANS 4:6-7

God, you protect my heart and my mind. You bring me perfect peace whenever I ask for it.

I am anxious today, Father. Life is exciting but scary right now. A good chapter has closed, and now I am embarking on a new beginning. Give me the kind of peace that only you can give.

I pray right now for everything this new beginning will bring. Protect my insecurities from anxious thoughts.

Thank you for the opportunity to try new things in life.

In Jesus' name, amen.

195

And the LORD He is the One who goes before you.
He will be with you, He will not leave you nor
forsake you; do not fear not be dismayed.

DEUTERONOMY 31:8

Father, you are faithful. You never leave me. Wherever I am, you are there too.

God, help me be strong, and help me have courage. Don't let worry get in the way of my being joyful and excited about this fresh start.

Be with the people I am leaving. Even though we are not together as much now, remind them that you are always with them.

Thank you for your presence in my life every day.

In your name I pray, amen.

196

Stress and strain have caught up with me,
but your commandments are my joy!

PSALM 119:143 CEB

Heavenly Father, you are the creator of this world and all its beauty. You are the God who sees me and the one who made me just for this time and place.

When I am stressed , please give me your peace. Replace the shallow reassurances of the world with your holy presence so my heart will be calm.

Bring peace to my family and friends too. Stifle stress with your joy. Give us a positive outlook on the future, and keep us from being pessimistic.

In a world where daily life is often measured by our stress levels, thank you for providing the calm that is beyond all understanding.

In your majestic name, amen.

197

Let the peace of God rule in your hearts, to which
also you were called in one body; and be thankful.

COLOSSIANS 3:15

Father, you are the God of peace that surpasses all understanding.

When possible conflicts arise with others, remind me to be thoughtful in my response, to respond as you would. Remind me of the importance of being a peacemaker because I am part of the body of Christ. Keep me from the sin of arguing and instead help me focus on loving those around me.

God, bless my community with peace, and help me speak words of kindness to others. Remind me to encourage those around me and to use words of respect with everyone I meet.

Thank you for the joy of human relationships. Thank you for sending the Prince of Peace for us all.

In his name, amen.

198

You are a hiding place for me;
You preserve me from trouble;
You surround me with shouts of deliverance.

PSALM 32:7 ESV

Almighty God, you are powerful. You possess all authority over heaven and earth.

This world can be a scary place. Please blanket our neighborhoods with your hand of protection. Keep us safe from those who do evil. Infuse us all with your calming peace. Replace fear with the power of your love.

Protect my family from harm. Protect my friends and coworkers, and prompt them to look to you for peace in times of trouble.

Thank you for being the God who loves us enough to protect our souls for all eternity through your Son, Jesus.

In his glorious name, amen.

199

For everyone who has been born of God
overcomes the world. And this is the victory
that has overcome the world—our faith.

1 JOHN 5:4 ESV

God, you are our rock and our salvation. In you we trust completely, for you are the mighty conqueror who has overcome the world!

When tragedy strikes, whether it affects our homes, our families, our friends, or our communities, protect us from anger and retaliation. You have loved us enough to overcome sin and conquer death.

When the people around us struggle to understand, provide peace, comfort, and the blessing of your grace. Remind us of your powerful words of reassurance in Scripture, so we may dwell there.

Thank you for wrapping your loving arms around us. Thank you for being our rock and for providing eternal life so that someday all sadness and evil will end.

In your Son's perfect name, amen.

200

Blessed is the man
Who walks not in the counsel of the ungodly,
Nor stands in the path of sinners,
Nor sits in the seat of the scornful;
But his delight is in the law of the LORD,
And in His law he meditates day and night.

PSALM 1:1-2

Father, you are the mighty lawgiver, and you alone are worthy of worship!

Help me protect my circle of friends and family. Give me the courage to fight for what is right on their behalf and to be an example of truth. Teach me your law so well that I can recognize when I need to defend the defenseless.

Protect our young children, Lord. They are exposed to so much ugliness early in their lives. Shield their minds, keep their thoughts clean, and help them choose good over evil. Give them wisdom, and meet their basic needs so they can focus on learning.

Thank you for providing your law so we can always know right from wrong.

In your powerful name, amen.

201

You shall not hate your brother in your heart. You shall
surely rebuke your neighbor, and not bear sin because
of him. You shall not take vengeance, nor bear any
grudge against the children of your people, but you
shall love your neighbor as yourself: I am the LORD.

LEVITICUS 19:17–18

Lord, you are the salvation of the world. You are the
source of light and love for this world. Holy are you!

When I have to deal with difficult people, give me
words that will bring peace to the conversation. Help
me communicate directly and with a grace that glorifies
you. Calm my emotions and keep me far from anger.
Remind me of the possibility that I might be the difficult
one. Humble me, Father.

Bless everyone I communicate with, Lord. Give them
a willingness to listen and to respect my opinions. And
do the same in my heart: give me openness and accep-
tance and the willingness to listen carefully.

Thank you for your command to love. It reminds
me that I'm to treat everyone with grace, just as you offer
that grace to me.

In your precious name, amen.

202

Now may the Lord of peace Himself give you peace
always in every way. The Lord be with you all.

2 THESSALONIANS 3:16

Father, you are wise and all-knowing. You allow all things to happen in your perfect timing.

Please give me peace in the midst of this busy season. I sometimes feel pulled in so many directions by the needs all around me.

Surround my family in this time. May your peace bring us all peace, and may you create a calm environment in our home and neighborhood.

Thank you that you have gone before us in hectic times and for bringing order to the chaos when we need it most. Thank you for giving me time to hug my friends and family and show them what precious gifts they are to me.

In Jesus' name, amen.

203

The LORD will give strength to His people;
The LORD will bless His people with peace.

PSALM 29:11

God, you are my strength during hard times. Your grace is sufficient for me, and your power is made perfect in my weakness.

Today I feel spread thin and overcommitted. I don't have the strength in me to do what needs to be done. Give me the energy I need just for today. Give me time for rest and rejuvenation. And forgive me if my choices have led to this.

Protect my family as we run from one activity to the next. May my attitude be joyful, and may theirs be calm.

Thank you for going before our day and for your love, peace, and protection that sustain us.

In your Son's name I pray, amen.

204

You will keep him in perfect peace,
Whose mind is stayed on You,
Because he trusts in You.

ISAIAH 26:3

Dear God, your ways are perfect. Your will is good. You deserve all praise.

You have promised perfect peace to those who focus on you. Help me to keep my thoughts on you. When I rush ahead to the next plan or responsibility, bring me back to you and your goodness.

Help me fix my eyes on you when I experience fear or anxiety. Show me who you are so I can trust you more.

I am grateful for the gift of peace found in you. Thank you for the example of faith that I see in the lives of my friends and family.

In your precious name I pray, amen.

205

A man's heart plans his way,
but the LORD directs his steps.

PROVERBS 16:9

Father, you are above time. You know what will happen before it happens. You are the creator and ruler of all.

Steady my heart today as I make to-do lists. Direct my steps. Do not let me be overcome by anxiety and fear.

Direct the steps of my family today as well. Show them that your way truly is the best way, and give them a desire to do your will and a sense of peace.

Thank you for your steadfast love. Thank you for giving me time to play with my children and for the joy that it brings to us all. I'm so grateful for their laughter and hugs.

In your name I pray, amen.

206

For the kingdom of God is . . . righteousness and
peace and joy in the Holy Spirit. For he who serves
Christ in these things is acceptable to God.

ROMANS 14:17-18

My father in heaven, only you deserve all glory and praise. You are my source of joy, peace, and love.

I so often make my own schedule and try to be the ruler of my calendar, rather than consulting with you first. Help me remember to seek your will before making choices. Point me toward the things that please you. I want to draw near to you, God, and to do what is right in your eyes.

I will serve you today. Do not let distractions or the Enemy get in the way of my focus on you.

I am so grateful that I am not in charge of my own life. Thank you for your constant guidance.

In Jesus' name, amen.

207

So teach us to number our days,
That we may gain a heart of wisdom.

PSALM 90:12

Heavenly Father, only you know the number of my days. In your infinite wisdom you have a plan for each of your children, including me.

Remind me to live each day as if it's my last. Don't let me take a single moment for granted. May each of my actions be intentional during this time.

Be with my family today, Lord. Do not let them coast through this life; instead, give them an excitement for it and a deep joy that comes from you.

Thank you for caring about us and how we spend each day here on earth.

In Jesus' name I pray, amen.

208

Therefore do not worry about tomorrow, for
tomorrow will worry about its own things.
Sufficient for the day is its own trouble.

MATTHEW 6:34

God, you are a God who listens to his people. You hear when we call on you, and you don't ignore us.

Steady my thoughts today. My life feels so busy, and I have not had time to slow down. My mind is racing. Help me be focused in this moment.

Protect my family's thoughts today. Do not let them be filled with worry or fear but rather with your love, peace, and assurance.

Thank you for listening to me when I speak and for the confidence that your love gives me and my family.

In the precious name of your Son, I pray, amen.

PRAYERS *for* PERSEVERANCE AND ENDURANCE

209

Never be lacking in zeal, but keep your
spiritual fervor, serving the Lord.

ROMANS 12:11 NIV

Heavenly Father, your love is our banner and triumph. We rejoice in you!

You instilled a passion in me—a passion to help other people and to continue to learn from your teachings. God, keep the flames of that passion burning brightly. It's about sharing your love, your encouragement, and your passion for others.

Let me help others discover their talents or interests that drive their desire to learn and to seek a future as bright as your love and light.

Thank you for making me a constant student of your teachings. I love what I do, and I love you, Lord.

In Christ's name, amen.

210

You therefore must endure hardship as
a good soldier of Jesus Christ.

2 TIMOTHY 2:3

Heavenly Father, you have legions of angels at your command, and all the forces of nature serve you. Yet you still listen to and love your people.

The calling you have given me is not without serious challenges. Strengthen me to face each obstacle in a way that will honor you. Help me to serve you through the tough times. Increase my trust in your Word and assurances.

Be with my family wherever they may be. Anything that impacts me, impacts them. Remind them that you are in control at all times. Remove any fears or doubts and replace them with patience and faith.

Thank you for placing me in my circumstances. I am grateful you have prepared me to face anything that comes my way.

In Jesus' name, amen.

211

Peace I leave with you, My peace I give to you;
not as the world gives do I give to you. Let not
your heart be troubled, neither let it be afraid.

JOHN 14:27

Father, you are slow to anger, gracious in mercy, and abounding in love. You are worthy of all praise and honor.

I humbly ask for your peace in my life. The stressors in my life cause many sleepless nights and worries and concerns. Fill me with your peace, and reassure me that you are there and in control.

Comfort and bless my loved ones. They, too, have to endure many challenges. Calm their spirits, and focus their hearts on you.

Thank you for caring about every part of our lives and every member of our families. Thank you for the Holy Spirit, who is our great Comforter.

In Jesus' name, amen.

212

*Therefore confess your sins to each other and pray
for each other so that you may be healed. The prayer
of a righteous person is powerful and effective.*

JAMES 5:16 NIV

Father, you lead your people and hear their prayers. You know each of your sheep by name. You are the great and wonderful Shepherd.

Help me find a trustworthy prayer partner. Too often, I try to go it alone, and I'm reluctant to share my spiritual life with others. Please change my heart. Give me a passion to reach out to other Christians so we can pray for one another and seek your will together.

Help those in my community. Ignite a desire in them to know you. Use me, and raise up Christians in our midst. I pray that those who live around me will come to know you.

Thank you for putting people in our paths who can walk this road of faith with us. Thank you for all the believers worldwide. May your mighty name continue to spread throughout the earth.

In Jesus' holy name, amen.

213

The plans of the LORD stand firm forever, the
purposes of his heart through all generations.
Blessed is the nation whose God is the LORD,
the people he chose for his inheritance.

PSALM 33:11-12 NIV

Dear Father, from the beginning of time, you have planned the path your people would take. Your infinite mind thought of me long before I was born. I am humbled by your incredible love.

I struggle with doubts and fear about my future. I don't trust you nearly as much as I should. Please forgive me and reinforce my faith in you. Help me understand and believe that you are in control and have a good plan for me, my family, and my career.

Bless my family today. Help them know that all things rest in your hands and that you always have their best interests in mind. Don't let them fear the future.

Thank you for ordering our steps and guiding our way. I am thankful to know that your thoughts are always for our good.

In your Son's name, amen.

214

Then the apostles gathered to Jesus and told Him all things, both what they had done and what they had taught. And He said to them, "Come aside by yourselves to a deserted place and rest a while." For there were many coming and going, and they did not even have time to eat.

MARK 6:30–31

God, you are the giver of peace, the restorer of my soul.

When I am exhausted, give me rest. Help me know when I need to slow down and when I need to set aside time to recharge. If I'm tempted to take on too much, help me find the balance in life, and remind me that my relationship with you and my family must be my main priority.

Restore energy to my body, inspiration to my mind, and excitement to my soul. Protect me from the fatigue of overworking.

Thank you for the example of taking a break, Lord. Thank you for creating a day of rest and for urging us to take advantage of it.

In the name of Christ, amen.

215

I am persuaded that neither death nor life, nor angels nor principalities nor powers, nor things present nor things to come, nor height nor depth, nor any other created thing, shall be able to separate us from the love of God which is in Christ Jesus our Lord.

ROMANS 8:38–39

Lord, every believer rests securely in your love. No one can snatch a single soul from your powerful hand.

Remind me that nothing stands between us. Because of my sins and the world around me, I get discouraged and sometimes believe I have done too much for you to love me. Help me keep that lie out of my thoughts, and let the depth of your love sink into my mind and my heart so I will never doubt again.

Shower your peace and love on my family. Show them that your love covers them in every circumstance. Wrap your arms around them, and give them the confidence that they are always yours.

I am grateful you love us so much that nothing will ever come between us. Thank you for fighting for me and never giving up on me.

In Christ's name, amen.

216

My dear brothers and sisters, stand firm. Let
nothing move you. Always give yourselves
fully to the work of the Lord, because you know
that your labor in the Lord is not in vain.

1 CORINTHIANS 15:58 NIV

Heavenly Father, your eternal love knows no measure. You and your love are beyond what our minds can even imagine.

Sometimes I feel very discouraged when I spend hours planning and don't get the results I want. I hear a voice that calls me inadequate. Remind me that I'm more than adequate because of your love.

Help my peers understand your Word. Remind them that what they do is about so much more than reaching quotas and achieving benchmarks. Remind them that the hearts they touch are much more important than any measurable result.

Thank you for giving me the opportunity to touch the hearts of others. It's a gift I don't take for granted.

In Christ's holy name, amen.

217

The word of God is alive and active. Sharper than
any double-edged sword, it penetrates even to
dividing soul and spirit, joints and marrow; it
judges the thoughts and attitudes of the heart.

HEBREWS 4:12 NIV

My God, you are alive and always active. Not a single moment escapes you. Not one thought or deed goes unnoticed.

I often depend on my routine to get through the day. I need that cup of coffee, that soda, or that chocolate. But remind me that your Word is more powerful than any jolt of caffeine. Let your truth flow through me, giving me energy to get through each day. Let your power infuse me!

When those around me need your strength, bless them with energy that is beyond anything humans can create. Let them walk and run and not grow weary or faint.

Thank you for being all that I need.

In your name, amen.

218

*Brothers and sisters, we instructed you how
to live in order to please God, as in fact you
are living. Now we ask you and urge you in
the Lord Jesus to do this more and more.*

1 THESSALONIANS 4:1 NIV

Father in heaven, you are the giver of truth. You instruct me through your Word, and I want to keep learning.

Sometimes I feel unmotivated. I'm burned out from the daily grind and endless requirements. Remind me that life isn't about pleasing others but pleasing you. Give me fuel through your Word, and inspire me to live each moment for you.

When my friends or coworkers need motivation, let me be a cheerleader. When I need motivation, let them bring words of encouragement, so together we can create a positive culture that's contagious.

Thank you for others who work hard. Thank you for your example through Jesus Christ.

In his holy name, amen.

219

Count it all joy when you fall into various trials,
knowing that the testing of your faith produces
patience. But let patience have its perfect work, that
you may be perfect and complete, lacking nothing.

JAMES 1:2-4

God, your love can never be matched. Your every thought and desire are for our good. Each of your works is a blessing and a masterpiece.

Every day there seem to be new challenges to my faith. I often wonder if I can stand up to them, and sometimes I don't. Help the trials in my life to do their perfect work in me. Change my attitude toward difficulties and testing so I see they are there not to break me but to make me stronger, to build me up.

Fill my family with joy today as they work through their hardships. May they have fresh outlooks and transformed spirits.

Thank you for being our rock during the storms of life. Thank you for the promises you have made to us in your Word.

In your Son's holy name, amen.

220

If you faithfully obey the commands I am giving you
*today—to love the L*ORD *your God and to serve him with*
all your heart and with all your soul—then I will send rain
on your land in its season. . . . I will provide grass in the
fields for your cattle, and you will eat and be satisfied.

DEUTERONOMY 11:13–15 NIV

Most High God, you are unchanging. You are present in every moment of eternity.

On the days I am weary and weak, give me strength. Remind me that as long as I put you first in my life, you will give me the wisdom and encouragement I need to do my job and to see it as a gift.

God, remind me of your promises. Instill in me a hunger to do my job well. Lead others who may have lost their passion for their careers to their true callings so they may be blessed as you planned.

Thank you for revealing my calling through each and every person I've known.

In your name, amen.

221

For we walk by faith, not by sight.

2 CORINTHIANS 5:7

Jesus, how magnificent your name is in all the earth. A time will come when every knee will bow and every tongue will confess that you are Lord.

Help me walk in true faith. Too often I guide my life by my own pride and selfish desires. Teach me to trust you fully and to live according to your will. Give me the discipline and desire to search the Scriptures and to pray daily to know you better.

Draw my family and friends closer to you today. Reveal yourself to them, and help them grow in their faith. May they seek an authentic and active relationship with you.

Thank you for drawing us ever closer to you and being the light for our path. I am so very thankful to be your child.

In your name I pray, amen.

PRAYERS *for* RELATIONSHIP WITH GOD

222

I am the vine; you are the branches. If you
remain in me and I in you, you will bear much
fruit; apart from me you can do nothing.

— JOHN 15:5 NIV

Father, you pursue your children when they stray, and you run and embrace them when they return. Your grace and mercy are unending.

I too often allow myself to become separated from you, and I try to live my own way. Forgive me and keep my feet on the right path. Don't let any obstacles get in the way of my relationship with you. Help me to bear good fruit and to be useful to you. Keep me connected to you always.

I pray that my fellow believers will remain committed to you. Keep them close, and continue to pour your love and mercies on them. Bless my friends , family, and community. May your hand always protect them.

Thank you for keeping us close to you and helping us grow. I am grateful for your loving grace in my life.

In your holy name, amen.

223

He who says he abides in Him ought himself
also to walk just as He walked.

1 JOHN 2:6

Dear God, without you I am nothing. Without you I can do nothing. You are my everything—my strength, my joy, and my comfort.

Teach me what it means to abide in you. Strengthen my relationship with you. Bring me closer to you so I will walk with you every day and get to know you more and more.

I pray for the members of my family. I pray that each one will draw closer to you.

Thank you that I get to have a relationship with you, my God.

In Jesus' name, amen.

224

*Remember your leaders, who spoke the word
of God to you. Consider the outcome of their
way of life and imitate their faith.*

HEBREWS 13:7 NIV

Dear Father, you sent your Son, Jesus, to establish your church here on earth. You did not leave us alone because you care about us so much.

Help me find a church and a group of other Christians to worship with. Let it be a place that is safe, and let there be wise mentors to help guide me.

I pray for the leaders in my new church. Guide the pastors, ministers, and elders, and give them your wisdom.

Thank you for your church.

In Jesus' name I pray, amen.

225

Oh, how I love Your law!
It is my meditation all the day.

PSALM 119:97

F ather, your law is love, and your love is so strong I cannot understand it. You love your creation and everything that is in it.

Lord, remind me of your words when I wake up in the morning, when I go to sleep at night, and as I go about my day-to-day life. Write your words on my heart.

Help my family and friends, the ones who taught me about you and your love for me. Stay close to them, and remind them of your promises today.

Thank you for giving me your Word, which helps me know you better.

In Jesus' name, amen.

226

And let us consider one another in order to
stir up love and good works, not forsaking the
assembling of ourselves together, as is the manner
of some, but exhorting one another, and so much
the more as you see the Day approaching.

HEBREWS 10:24–25

Dear God, you are my faithful Father. You are so good to me. Everything you do is righteous and for your glory.

I need help finding a Christian community. Would you put people in my life who will encourage me, and help me encourage others?

I pray for the people who do ministry in this community. I pray they will feel strengthened by those around them.

Thank you that we are never alone in our Christian walk.

In Christ I pray, amen.

227

For My flesh is food indeed, and My blood is
drink indeed. He who eats My flesh and drinks
My blood abides in Me, and I in him. As the living
Father sent Me, and I live because of the Father,
so he who feeds on Me will live because of Me.

JOHN 6:55–57

Dear God, you really are all that I need. You are the answer to all my questions. You are my hope when I feel hopeless.

Please forgive me for looking to other people and other things to fulfill me or make me happy. I want to serve only you. Bring me back to you, God.

Help my friends who are not following you right now but have started going after empty, worldly things. Remind them that you are what they need.

I am so grateful you are my God and my Father and my faithful guide.

In Jesus' name, amen.

228

For by wise guidance you can wage your war,
and in an abundance of counselors there is victory.

PROVERBS 24:6 ESV

Dear God, you are a wise and good Father. Nothing matters more in my life than you. I am grateful for your love and grace.

I ask for your wisdom today, God. I need it more than ever now. Give me wise friends who love you and will encourage my relationship with you.

I pray for my friends who are in the same phase of life as I am. Please bring mentors to encourage them along the way.

Thank you for being so close to me during this time. In Jesus' holy name, amen.

229

Then Jesus said to those Jews who believed Him, "If you abide in My word, you are My disciples indeed. And you shall know the truth, and the truth shall make you free."

JOHN 8:31–32

Dear God, your Word is true. It is powerful and life changing.

Please give me more passion for your Word. Help me to set aside time each day to read Scripture and consider what you want me to receive from the reading. Let your Word speak to me, change me, correct and comfort me. Be with those people who don't have Bibles in their homes or even in their countries. I pray for their souls and their hearts that long to know you. I pray your Word will come to them in ways only you could orchestrate.

Thank you for giving us your Word, which is true every day.

In Christ's name, amen.

PRAYERS *for* REST

230

For you did not receive
the spirit of bondage again to fear,
but you received
the Spirit of adoption by whom we cry out,
"Abba, Father."

ROMANS 8:15

Father, you have made me your child through your Spirit. In your kindness you adopted me and delivered me from sin and death.

Remind me today what it means to be your child. It is so easy for me to live my day on my own terms. Help me to live it in light of your grace.

I pray for my friends and family. Help them rest in your love as their Father and feel their inheritance in your Spirit.

Thank you for accepting me as I am but not leaving me the same.

In Jesus' name, amen.

231

Our Father in heaven,
Hallowed be Your name.
Your kingdom come.
Your will be done
On earth as it is in heaven.

MATTHEW 6:9–10

Father, you are above all, know all, and see all. Yet you hear me as if I were your only creation.

May I not view you as a distant father but as one who has come to earth and understands the challenges and temptations of my life. Be near me today and whisper reminders that you are close and holding me as your child. Help me to rest in your love.

My friends need you today as they make difficult decisions in their workplaces and within their families. Would you show them that you are closer than even their earthly fathers? Please provide them with the rest they need.

Thank you for hearing me and listening to my pleas.

It's in Jesus' name I pray this, amen.

232

Yet for us there is one God, the Father, of
whom are all things, and we for Him; and
one Lord Jesus Christ, through whom are
all things, and through whom we live.

1 CORINTHIANS 8:6

God, you are my Father who gives all good things.
I have life because of you, and there is no one
like you.

I ask that you would deepen that truth in my heart
today. Point out the things I worship apart from you, that
I would remember you alone are my God.

Give my friends and loved ones freedom from their
idols as well so they can fully enjoy being part of your
family. Help them rest in the knowledge that you are
their only creator, and nothing on this earth has own-
ership of them.

Thank you for loving us, your creation, even when
we go astray.

In Jesus' name, amen.

233

A father of the fatherless, a defender of widows,
Is God in His holy habitation.
God sets the solitary in families;
He brings out those who are bound into prosperity.

PSALM 68:5–6

Dear God, you are the Father to the fatherless. You provide for those without a family and defend the weak as their own father would.

Today I feel defenseless. When I feel attacked, would you remind me that you protect me? Would you be my Father and defender today?

Please defend those who are weak and afraid and feel forgotten. Show up in their lives today and remind them that they are your children and you are their heavenly Father. Provide the rest they need to see things clearly.

Thank you for giving me a spiritual family that can never be taken away.

I pray this in the name of Jesus, amen.

234

Hear my cry, O God;
Attend to my prayer.
From the end of the earth I will cry to You,
When my heart is overwhelmed;
Lead me to the rock that is higher than I.

PSALM 61:1–2

Father in heaven, you are the God of King David and my God too. You reign forever and over everything.

Bring me peace when I am overwhelmed. I don't know how I can accomplish all the things I need to get done. Light my path and show me the activities and obligations I can say no to. Help me release the burdens that preoccupy my mind and keep you at bay. Come near.

God, please hear the cries of those who feel overwhelmed as they serve you. Many of them don't feel your presence right now in their lives. Remind them of your faithfulness.

Thank you for your nearness and consistency and the rest they provide. Thank you for hearing my cries no matter where I am.

In Jesus' name, amen.

235

*Who being the brightness of His glory and the express
image of His person, and upholding all things by the
word of His power, when He had by Himself purged our
sins, sat down at the right hand of the Majesty on high,
having become so much better than the angels, as He has
by inheritance obtained a more excellent name than they.*

HEBREWS 1:3-4

Father, you created all things simply with your words.
One word from you and your power is evident. I am
amazed by you.

I need your power in my life, God. I need the strength
and rest it brings. I face impossible circumstances and
am desperate for a miracle. Would you show me your
power in my life today?

God, for those who have a small view of you, show
them how mighty and enormous you actually are. Help
them to find rest and comfort in that knowledge.

Thank you for sending your Son, who has made our
relationship with you possible.

It's in the all-powerful name of Jesus that I pray,
amen.

236

"For I am God, and there is no other;
I am God, and there is none like Me,
Declaring the end from the beginning,
And from ancient times things that are not yet done,
Saying, My counsel shall stand,
And I will do all My pleasure."

ISAIAH 46:9–10

God above, there is no one like you. You are the one, true God. The only God that I worship, the Alpha and Omega.

I need to know that you have gone before me. I see no solution for the problems I'm facing. Remind me that you are not perplexed by the struggles I face so that I may rest and be comforted by your all-knowing power.

Be near to my family and friends who are suffering. Their pain is paralyzing, but you are greater than anything they face.

Thank you for your perfect will. May it be done in my life as I seek you.

In your name alone, amen.

237

For unto us a Child is born
Unto us a Son is given;
And the government will be upon His shoulder.
And His name will be called
Wonderful, Counselor, Mighty God,
Everlasting Father, Prince of Peace.

ISAIAH 9:6

Dear Father, you are the Prince of Peace and the great I AM. You are my helper and my redeemer.

I need your help today. I am weak and frail and tired. Give me the strength to get through just this day and the desire to work as if I am doing it all for your glory.

Help those who are carrying especially heavy burdens right now. They need your power and peace that goes beyond our understanding.

I am so grateful that I can come to you and present my requests at any time. Thank you for giving me peace and rest even in the hard times.

In the name of the Prince of Peace, I pray, amen.

Therefore humble yourselves under the mighty hand
of God, that He may exalt you in due time, casting
all your care upon Him, for He cares for you.
1 PETER 5:6–7

Dear God, you are above all and worthy is your name. I humbly come before you, confessing that I am a sinner. What I have done deserves justice and not grace, but I need to feel your grace today. I need your forgiveness. Would you replace the guilt, replace the shame I feel?

Be near to my friends and family who have secret shame they are afraid to reveal. May you give them a trusted friend and confidant and a sense of your forgiveness in their lives.

Thank you for taking our cares and burdens upon yourself. Thank you for promising to always care for each of us. Thank you for listening, so I can rest easy in your love.

In Jesus' name, amen.

239

For to You, O Lord, I lift up my soul.
For You, Lord, are good, and ready to forgive,
And abundant in mercy to all those who call upon You.

PSALM 86:4–5

God, you are abounding in forgiveness and mercy and goodness I cannot understand in this life. I worship you with my heart and soul.

As I sit in regret and guilt over past sin, remind me of your forgiveness. Please let me feel your mercy and rest in your faithfulness. Fill me with it so I can give it to others I encounter today.

Walk closely with my friends and family so they can know your grace. Lift their burdens and point their faces toward you.

I give you thanks for the grace I do not deserve and your mercies, which are new every morning.

In Christ's name, amen.

PRAYERS *for*
WISDOM AND
LEADERSHIP

240

*If any of you lacks wisdom, you should ask
God, who gives generously to all without
finding fault, and it will be given to you.*

JAMES 1:5 NIV

Heavenly Father, you are the fountain of all that is good, right, and true. Your knowledge is limitless, and your understanding is without equal.

I humbly ask for wisdom, Lord. I need help living according to your instructions. Direct my understanding and knowledge. Show me what is right in your eyes, and give me the desire to stay on the path you have for me. Help me discipline myself to study your Word regularly.

Let my family's goal be to know your thoughts and plans for their lives. Place your Word in their hearts, and make it the foundation for their lives. Give them the joy of knowing you better.

I am extremely grateful that you have given us your instruction manual. Thank you for allowing us insight into your character, plan, and wisdom.

In Jesus' name, amen.

241

The way of a fool is right in his own eyes,
But he who heeds counsel is wise.

PROVERBS 12:15

Lord, you raise up nations, and you bring them low. You make kings, and you remove them from their thrones. The entire world is subject to your good and merciful will.

Help me find good mentors and friends, who will speak wisdom into my life. Reveal to me a good adviser at work so I can serve my community well and excel in my job. Let me always be a seeker of your perfect ways.

Guide my family to choose wisely those they seek counsel from and those they associate with. As they surround themselves with godly people and leaders, strengthen their fellowship and friendship.

Thank you for Christian community. I am grateful for the many people you have placed in my life who have had a great influence on me.

In Christ's name, amen.

242

Whoever desires to become great among
you, let him be your servant.

MATTHEW 20:26

God, you command the power of life and death. You hold the stars and planets in place. Your power and majesty astound me.

I want to know how to be a good leader and role model. Please help me understand how to be a good servant leader. Keep me humble and my motives pure. Give me the wisdom and the heart to care for the people I lead. Develop my spirit so I will earn the respect of those I work with.

Bless my friends and show yourself to them. Protect them from harm and place angels around them.

I am thankful that you have given us godly examples of leadership. Thank you for instilling in me the yearning to lead and serve.

In Jesus' name, amen.

243

*To the person who pleases him, God gives
wisdom, knowledge and happiness.*

ECCLESIASTES 2:26 NIV

Heavenly Father, you have the power to bring life out of death. You breathe your very Spirit into us. You are the one and only true God.

Lord, I am asking you to bless me with this promise. I am humbly seeking your wisdom to lead my family, guide my life, and direct my career. I am also asking that you give me the understanding to serve you with all my heart, mind, strength, and talents.

My family desires your wisdom and guidance for their lives too. Bless them with your knowledge and grace today.

Thank you for loving us so much that you're willing to teach us everything we need to know. Thank you for being so generous with your knowledge and wisdom.

In Jesus' name, amen.

244

Let your "Yes" be "Yes,"
and your "No," "No."
MATTHEW 5:37

Father, you are without error or blemish. You are perfect in all your ways, and the works of your hands are flawless. The heavens declare your glory.

Help me be a person of conviction and truth. Teach me to always keep my word so I can be trusted in everything I say and do. Let those who work with me know I will always seek to follow your Word when I am in charge. Reveal to me any character issues or weaknesses I need to address.

Watch over my coworkers, friends, and family, and if they don't know you, bring them into a saving knowledge of your Son.

Thank you for showing us the way of godly leadership. Thank you for encouraging me to excel.

In Jesus' name, amen.

245

Do I now persuade men, or God? Or do I seek
to please men? For if I still pleased men, I
would not be a bondservant of Christ.

GALATIANS 1:10

Almighty God, you hear my cries and comfort me. Your loving grace has wrapped itself around my heart. I am so blessed to be your child.

Sometimes I worry more about what people think than what your Word tells me. I often feel as if my feet are planted in two separate worlds. Please forgive me and help me be more obedient to you. Guide me to walk in your ways without shame or wavering. Help me be bold for you and the truth of your Word.

Infuse my family with faith and confidence. Clear out the distractions and obstacles in our home that hinder your work there. Help us set the right priorities, and teach us not to compromise on your Word and what we know to be true.

Thank you for your patience and grace. I am so grateful for the incredible blessings you have given our family.

In Jesus' holy name, amen.

246

Show me Your ways, O Lord;
Teach me Your paths.
Lead me in Your truth and teach me,
For You are the God of my salvation;
On You I wait all the day.

PSALM 25:4–5

G od, your ways are wise and true. Your decrees breathe life into your people. You are a God who forever directs their steps.

I confess that I have not studied your Word as much as I should. I want to know you more and be led by you. I want to guide my family and run my home by your loving instructions. Give me the discipline to study your Word and the ears to hear your voice. Show me, Lord.

Open my children's eyes to you today. They are growing quickly. Before too long they will be off to college or on their own. Please capture their hearts now and walk with them through the rest of their lives.

Thank you for giving us your Word so we may know you. Thank you for protecting us from ourselves with your instructions.

In your holy name, amen.

247

Trust in the LORD with all your heart,
And lean not on your own understanding;
In all your ways acknowledge Him,
And He shall direct your paths.

PROVERBS 3:5–6

Heavenly Father, you are the same today, tomorrow, and forever. Your loving character and holiness are unchangeable.

I really struggle with trusting you in every aspect of my life. I constantly want to take control and work things out myself. Forgive me. Help me acknowledge you first and to look for your direction. I want to have your insight and wisdom in all I do.

Bless my family today. As we praise you together, direct our lives. Blaze a careful path for each of us, and guide us along that path to you. Teach us to rely on you for all things.

I am so grateful for the family and friends you have given me. Thank you for your constant desire to gently direct our way.

In Christ's name, amen.

248

*Jesus, knowing that the Father had given all
things into His hands, and that He had come
from God and was going to God, rose from supper
and laid aside His garments, took a towel and
girded Himself. After that, He poured water into
a basin and began to wash the disciples' feet.*

JOHN 13:3–5

Lord, despite having all the power and majesty of
God, you still chose to be with your creation and
even to serve us. Your love, mercy, and grace are beyond
comprehension.

When I think of leading my family or others, please
remind me of this scripture. Give me the heart of a servant leader. Humble my spirit so I will desire to serve as
you served, to lead as you led.

Let your humility pour onto my friends and family, and guide them with your example. Don't let them
become too focused on themselves and their desires.

Thank you that you are so powerful and yet so gentle
with your people. I am grateful that you show yourself to
us in many different ways.

In Jesus' name, amen.

249

*Shepherd the flock of God which is among you, serving
as overseers, not by compulsion but willingly, not for
dishonest gain but eagerly; nor as being lords over
those entrusted to you, but being examples to the
flock; and when the Chief Shepherd appears, you will
receive the crown of glory that does not fade away.*

1 PETER 5:2-4

God, your righteous love drives away fear and sin.
Your thoughts and will are always for our good.
You are the true and perfect Father.

I want to be the family member that you created me
to be. Help me study your Word so I can love my family
gently and with wisdom. Keep me from my selfish
desires and foolish decisions.

Direct my family and friends as they go through
their days. Keep your angels near them. Stir their hearts
to love one another and to be kind to others. Help them
appreciate their many blessings.

Thank you for teaching me how to love my family
and friends. I am grateful I have your Word and your
Spirit to guide me.

In your name, amen.

250

You shall select from all the people able men, such
as fear God, men of truth, hating covetousness; and
place such over them to be rulers of thousands, rulers
of hundreds, rulers of fifties, and rulers of tens.

EXODUS 18:21

Heavenly Father, I am so in awe of you and how you take care of all of us. Every day I discover something new to worship about you.

Create in me the character I need to be a leader. I often feel that I am not worthy of my job and my responsibilities. Please grow my character so I am able to lead those around me and earn their respect. Teach me through your Word the lessons I need.

Let the principles of this scripture take hold in our environment. Encourage our leaders to pursue your character and will. Watch over our leaders that they will not be swayed by their personal desires. Teach them your ways.

Thank you for appointing those in charge and preparing their hearts for leadership.

In Jesus' name, amen.

MAX LUCADO

Available June 2022

They Walked with God takes a closer look at forty of the most inspirational characters in the Bible and shares a powerful message: if God can find a place for each character in the Bible, he's carved out a spot for you too.

WWW.MAXLUCADO.COM